INTRODUCTION

On December 23, 2024, the US House Ethics Committee released its years-long investigation into the illicit activities of former Rep. Matt Gaetz. In its findings, detailed evidence suggest that the former congressman engaged in various illicit activities involving women, minors, impermissible gifts, and obstruction of Congress, to name a few.

The 42-page report highlights its findings and provides factual background of incidences with key witnesses. It also discusses why the report was released by the House Ethics Committee, as well as the views of its chairman Michael Guest, who dissented to its release.

Matt Gaetz has vacated his seat in Congress prior to the report's release. He has sought a restraining order against the House Ethics Committee. He has also accused the House Ethics Committee of violating its own standards by releasing the report on a private citizen, since he was no longer a member of Congress. In his public remarks, he says his actions were "…embarrassing, though not criminal, that I probably partied, womanized, drank, and smoked more than I should have earlier in life…."

ADOPTED BY THE COMMITTEE ON ETHICS ON DECEMBER 10, 2024

118TH CONGRESS, 2ND SESSION
U.S. HOUSE OF REPRESENTATIVES
COMMITTEE ON ETHICS

IN THE MATTER OF ALLEGATIONS RELATING TO
REPRESENTATIVE MATT GAETZ

December 23, 2024

Mr. Guest from the Committee on Ethics, submitted the following

**REPORT
with DISSENTING VIEWS**

COMMITTEE ON ETHICS

MICHAEL GUEST, Mississippi
Chairman
DAVID P. JOYCE, Ohio
JOHN H. RUTHERFORD, Florida
ANDREW R. GARBARINO, New York
MICHELLE FISCHBACH, Minnesota

SUSAN WILD, Pennsylvania
Ranking Member
VERONICA ESCOBAR, Texas
MARK DESAULNIER, California
DEBORAH K. ROSS, North Carolina
GLENN F. IVEY, Maryland

REPORT STAFF

THOMAS A. RUST, *Chief Counsel / Staff Director*
BRITTNEY PESCATORE, *Director of Investigations*
KEELIE BROOM, *Counsel to the Chairman*
DAVID ARROJO, *Counsel to the Ranking Member*

SYDNEY R. BELLWOAR, *Senior Counsel*
MELISSA CHONG, *Counsel*
PEYTON WILMER, *Investigative Clerk*

CONTENTS

I. INTRODUCTION 1

II. PROCEDURAL HISTORY 3

III. RELEVANT LAWS, RULES, AND OTHER APPLICABLE STANDARDS OF CONDUCT 7

    A. Federal Laws 7

    B. Florida State Laws 8

    C. House Rules and Other Standards of Conduct 8

IV. FACTUAL BACKGROUND 10

    A. Allegations of Sexual Misconduct and Drug Use 10

    B. Allegations Relating to the House Gift Rule 25

    C. Allegations Related to Misuse of Official Resources 25

    D. Obstruction of the Committee's Investigation 26

V. FINDINGS 30

    A. The Committee Found Representative Gaetz Violated State Laws Related to Sexual Misconduct 30

    B. The Committee Found Representative Gaetz Used Illegal Drugs 32

    C. The Committee Found that Representative Gaetz Violated the House Gift Rule. 33

    D. The Committee Found Representative Gaetz Dispensed Special Privileges and Favors to Individuals with Whom He Had a Personal Relationship 34

    E. The Committee Found Representative Gaetz Sought to Obstruct Its Investigation of His Conduct 34

VI. CONCLUSION 36

VII. STATEMENT UNDER HOUSE RULE XIII, CLAUSE 3(c) 36

VIII. VIEWS OF CHAIRMAN MICHAEL GUEST ON BEHALF OF THE DISSENTING COMMITTEE MEMBERS 37

APPENDIX A: REPRESENTATIVE GAETZ'S CORRESPONDENCE WITH THE COMMITTEE
APPENDIX B: EXHIBITS TO THE COMMITTEE REPORT

118TH CONGRESS, 2ND SESSION
U.S. HOUSE OF REPRESENTATIVES
COMMITTEE ON ETHICS

IN THE MATTER OF ALLEGATIONS RELATING TO
REPRESENTATIVE MATT GAETZ

December 23, 2024

Mr. GUEST, from the Committee on Ethics, submitted the following

REPORT
with
DISSENTING VIEWS

In accordance with House Rule XI, clauses 3(a)(2) and 3(b), the Committee on Ethics (Committee) hereby submits the following Report to the House of Representatives, including the Views of Chairman Guest on behalf of the dissenting Committee Members:

I. INTRODUCTION

On April 9, 2021, the Committee announced it was investigating a series of widely reported allegations relating to Representative Matt Gaetz. At the request of the Department of Justice (DOJ), the Committee deferred its review during the 117th Congress. After it was organized for the 118th Congress, the Committee reauthorized its investigation into the allegations involving Representative Gaetz. Specifically, the Committee undertook a review of allegations that Representative Gaetz may have: engaged in sexual misconduct and/or illicit drug use; shared inappropriate images or videos on the House floor; misused state identification records; converted campaign funds to personal use; and/or accepted a bribe, improper gratuity, or impermissible gift. In June 2024, following extensive factfinding, the Committee determined to continue its review of the allegations of sexual misconduct, illicit drug use, and acceptance of impermissible gifts and expanded its review to include allegations that Representative Gaetz may have dispensed special privileges and favors to individuals with whom he had a personal relationship and obstructed government investigations into his conduct. At that time, the Committee determined to take no further action on the allegations relating to the House floor, state identification records, personal use of campaign funds, and acceptance of a bribe or gratuity.

On November 14, 2024, Representative Gaetz resigned from the House, after the President-Elect announced his intention to nominate Representative Gaetz for the position of United States Attorney General. As a result of Representative Gaetz's resignation, the Committee lost jurisdiction to continue its investigation. Representative Gaetz subsequently withdrew from consideration for the position of Attorney General; at this time, he has not announced any intent to seek higher office or return to Congress.

The Committee has typically not released its findings after losing jurisdiction in a matter.[1] However, there are a few prior instances where the Committee has determined that it was in the public interest to release its findings even after a Member's resignation from Congress.[2] The Committee does not do so lightly. In this instance, although several Committee Members objected, a majority of the Members of the Committee agreed that the Committee's findings should be released to the public.

In sum, the Committee found substantial evidence of the following:

- From at least 2017 to 2020, Representative Gaetz regularly paid women for engaging in sexual activity with him.
- In 2017, Representative Gaetz engaged in sexual activity with a 17-year-old girl.
- During the period 2017 to 2019, Representative Gaetz used or possessed illegal drugs, including cocaine and ecstasy, on multiple occasions.
- Representative Gaetz accepted gifts, including transportation and lodging in connection with a 2018 trip to the Bahamas, in excess of permissible amounts.
- In 2018, Representative Gaetz arranged for his Chief of Staff to assist a woman with whom he engaged in sexual activity in obtaining a passport, falsely indicating to the U.S. Department of State that she was a constituent.
- Representative Gaetz knowingly and willfully sought to impede and obstruct the Committee's investigation of his conduct.
- Representative Gaetz has acted in a manner that reflects discreditably upon the House.

Based on the above, the Committee concluded there was substantial evidence that Representative Gaetz violated House Rules, state and federal laws, and other standards of conduct prohibiting prostitution, statutory rape, illicit drug use, acceptance of impermissible gifts, the provision of special favors and privileges, and obstruction of Congress.

The Committee did not find sufficient evidence to conclude that Representative Gaetz violated the federal sex trafficking statute. Although Representative Gaetz did cause the transportation of women across state lines for purposes of commercial sex, the Committee did not find evidence that any of those women were under 18 at the time of travel, nor did the Committee find sufficient evidence to conclude that the commercial sex acts were induced by force, fraud, or coercion.

---

[1] *See, e.g.*, Statements of the Chair and Ranking Member in the Matters of Representative Jeff Fortenberry (Apr. 1, 2022), Duncan Hunter (Jan. 14, 2020), Chris Collins (Oct. 1, 2019), Chaka Fattah (June, 24, 2016), Henry "Trey" Radel (Jan. 29, 2014).
[2] *See, e.g.*, Comm. on Standards of Official Conduct, *In the Matter of Representative Daniel J. Flood*, H. Rept. 96-856, 96th Cong., 2d. Sess. (1980); Staff Report of the Comm. on Standards of Official Conduct, *In the Matter of Representative Donald E. Lukens* (1990); Staff Report of the Comm. on Standards of Official Conduct, *In the Matter of Representative William H. Boner* (1987).

Representative Gaetz was uncooperative throughout the Committee's review. He provided minimal documentation in response to the Committee's requests. He also did not agree to a voluntary interview. On July 11, 2024, the Committee issued a subpoena to Representative Gaetz for his testimony. He did not appear, despite having received notice of the date and time of the deposition. The Committee then sent Representative Gaetz a set of written questions, to which he issued a public response that ignored most of the direct questions about his misconduct and mischaracterized the Committee's investigation and his participation up to that point. Despite Representative Gaetz's claims to the contrary, the Committee's singular mission is to protect the integrity of the House. When faced with serious public allegations against a Member, the Committee will often investigate, and when such allegations are false, the Committee has a shared goal with the respondent to disprove those allegations.

While the Committee considered whether to establish an investigative subcommittee to consider sanctions against Representative Gaetz, the Committee ultimately determined that it would not risk the further victimization of the women involved in this matter. Most of the women with whom the Committee spoke also gave statements to DOJ and urged the Committee to rely on those statements in lieu of requiring them to relive their experience. They were particularly concerned with providing additional testimony about a sitting congressman in light of DOJ's lack of action on their prior testimony. DOJ refused to provide the relevant statements and other significant evidence to the Committee. DOJ cited internal policies about protecting uncharged subjects like Representative Gaetz, general concerns about how DOJ's cooperation with the Committee may deter other victims in other matters, and various inapposite policies relating to congressional oversight of DOJ itself. DOJ's initial deferral request and subsequent lack of cooperation with the Committee's review caused significant delays in the investigation; those delays were compounded by Representative Gaetz's obstructive efforts. The Committee has determined that its findings must be released without further impediments.

Accordingly, on December 10, 2024, the Committee voted on whether to release this Report; although several Members did not support its release, a majority of the Members voted in favor of its release.

II. PROCEDURAL HISTORY

On April 9, 2021, the Committee publicly announced it was investigating allegations relating to Representative Gaetz, including whether he may have: engaged in sexual misconduct and/or illicit drug use; shared inappropriate images or videos on the House floor; misused state identification records; converted campaign funds to personal use; and/or accepted a bribe, improper gratuity, or impermissible gift.[3] Shortly thereafter, DOJ requested that the Committee defer all investigation of Representative Gaetz. The Committee did so.

---

[3] Comm. on Ethics, Statement of the Chairman and Ranking Member of the Committee on Ethics Regarding Representative Matt Gaetz (Apr. 9, 2021), https://ethics.house.gov/press-releases/statement-chairman-and-ranking-member-committee-ethics-regarding-representative-22. The Committee's well-established precedent is to publicly announce its investigations when there are public allegations of sexual misconduct. *See, e.g.*, Comm. on Ethics, Statement of the Chairwoman and Ranking Member of the Committee on Ethics Regarding Representative John Conyers, Jr. (Nov. 21, 2017), https://ethics.house.gov/press-release/statement-chairwoman-and-ranking-member-

In February 2023, after the Committee asked DOJ for an update on its deferral request, public reports indicated that DOJ had informed Representative Gaetz and multiple witnesses that the congressman would not be charged in connection with the investigation. Shortly thereafter, DOJ informed the Committee it was no longer requesting a deferral. The Chairman and Ranking Member reauthorized the matter in May of 2023 in accordance with Committee Rule 18(a).[4]

On June 18, 2024, the Committee announced that the scope of the inquiry would focus on allegations of sexual misconduct, illicit drug use, acceptance of improper gifts, dispensation of special privileges and favors to individuals with whom he had a personal relationship, and obstruction of government investigations. At that time, the Committee also stated it would not continue to investigate allegations of sharing inappropriate images or videos on the House floor, misusing state identification records, converting campaign funds to personal use, and accepting a bribe or improper gratuity.

The Chairman and Ranking Member sent nine requests for information and six Freedom of Information Act (FOIA) requests.[5] The Committee also authorized 29 subpoenas for documents and testimony, reviewed nearly 14,000 documents, and contacted more than two dozen witnesses. The Committee also received sworn written responses from an associate of Representative Gaetz, Joel Greenberg; as discussed further below, however, the Committee determined that, due to

---

committee-ethics-regarding-representative-jo-1; Comm. on Ethics, Statement of the Chairwoman and Ranking Member of the Committee on Ethics Regarding Representative Ruben Kihuen (Dec. 15, 2017), https://ethics.house.gov/press-release/statement-chairwoman-and-ranking-member-committee-ethics-regarding-representative-8; Comm. on Ethics, Statement of the Chairwoman and Ranking Member of the Committee on Ethics Regarding Representative Patrick Meehan (Jan. 22, 2018), https://ethics.house.gov/press-release/statement-chairwoman-and-ranking-member-committee-ethics-regarding-representative-12; Comm. on Ethics, Statement of the Chairman and Ranking Member of the Committee on Ethics Regarding Delegate Michael F.Q. San Nicolas (Oct. 24, 2019), https://ethics.house.gov/press-releases/statement-chairman-and-ranking-member-committee-ethics-regarding-delegate-michael-f-q; Comm. on Ethics, Statement of the Chairman and Ranking Member Regarding Representative Katie Hill (Oct. 23, 2019), https://ethics.house.gov/press-releases/statement-chairman-and-ranking-member-committee-ethics-regarding-representative-katie; Comm. on Ethics, Statement of the Chairman and Ranking Member of the Committee on Ethics Regarding Representative Alcee Hastings (Nov. 14, 2019), https://ethics.house.gov/press-releases/statement-chairman-and-ranking-member-committee-ethics-regarding-representative-alcee; Comm. on Ethics, Statement of the Chairman and Ranking Member of the Committee on Ethics Regarding Representative Tom Reed (Apr. 9, 2021), https://ethics.house.gov/press-releases/statement-chairman-and-ranking-member-committee-ethics-regarding-representative-tom.

[4] The Committee typically reauthorizes unresolved matters at the start of a new Congress. It is also the Committee's longstanding practice to continue a deferred investigation after DOJ concludes a parallel review, even where DOJ declined to press charges. *See* Comm. on Ethics, *Summary of Activities for the One Hundred Fifteenth Congress*, H. Rept. 115-1125, 115th Cong., 2d Sess. 35 (2019) (noting the Committee deferred its investigation at the request of law enforcement and that the Committee had not closed its review of Representative Robert Pittenger after DOJ ended its investigation into the congressman); Comm. on Ethics, *In the Matter of Allegations Relating to Representative Vernon G. Buchanan*, H. Rept. 114-643, 114th Cong., 2d Sess. 2 (2016) (noting that the matter was "the subject of review by four different entities - the Committee, [Office of Congressional Ethics], [Federal Election Commission], and the Department of Justice" and that the DOJ investigation concluded in 2012); *cf. id* at 27 (noting that the Committee would not defer to decisions by other law enforcement agencies, including DOJ).

[5] Initially, the Chairman and Ranking Member sent only two voluntary requests for information, including the one to Representative Gaetz. After it became clear that Representative Gaetz was not cooperating in good faith, the Committee sought information from additional sources.

credibility issues, it would not rely exclusively on information provided by Mr. Greenberg in making any findings.

Shortly after DOJ withdrew its deferral request and the Committee reauthorized its review, the Committee sent DOJ a request for information. After three months without a response despite repeated follow up, the Committee submitted FOIA requests to several relevant DOJ offices, which to date have not been adequately processed.[6] The Committee continued to reach out to DOJ throughout 2023, having still not received a substantive response to its request for information. On January 12, 2024, the Committee received its first correspondence from DOJ on the matter. At that time, DOJ provided no substantive response or explanation for its delay; instead, DOJ simply stated that it "do[es] not provide non-public information about law enforcement investigations that do not result in charges."[7] This "policy" is, however, inconsistent with DOJ's historical conduct with respect to the Committee and its unique role in upholding the integrity of the House.[8]

Thereafter, the Committee determined to issue a subpoena to DOJ to obtain records relating to its investigation of Representative Gaetz. DOJ did not comply with the subpoena by the date required, but suggested it remained "committed to good-faith engagement with the Committee."[9] In the spirit of cooperation, the Committee provided a list of specific responsive documents, setting

---

[6] The U.S. Attorney's Office affirmatively declined the Committee's FOIA request as "categorically exempt from disclosure." However, the reasons cited for not disclosing responsive records are not applicable to the Committee's request—it did not consider the special access granted to Congress pursuant to 5 U.S.C. § 522(8)(d) (stating that FOIA "is not an authority to withhold information from Congress" even when an exemption may otherwise be implicated), nor did it consider the overriding public interest exception, which has been applied to information that would inform the public about proven violations of public trust (*see, e.g., Columbia Packing Co., Inc v. Department of Agriculture*, 564 F.3d 495, 499 (1st Cir. 1977) (federal employees found guilty of accepting bribes); *Congressional News Syndicate v. Department of Justice*, 438 F. Supp. 538, 544 (D.D.C. 1977) (misconduct by White House staffers)).

[7] Letter from U.S. Attorney's Office, U.S. Department of Justice, to Chairman Michael Guest and Ranking Member Susan Wild, Committee on Ethics (Jan. 12, 2024).

[8] Comm. on Ethics, *In the Matter of Representative Don Young*, H. Rept. 113-487, 113th Cong., 2d Sess. (2014) (hereinafter *Young*) (discussing information and documents provided to the Committee by DOJ relating to a Federal Bureau of Investigation (FBI) investigation of Representative Young); Comm. on Standards of Official Conduct, *In the Matter of Representative James McDermott*, H. Rept. 109-732, 109th Cong., 2d Sess. 5 (2006) (hereinafter *McDermott*) (noting that the investigative subcommittee requested and obtained documents from DOJ regarding its investigation of the matter); Comm. on Standards of Official Conduct, *In the Matter of Representative Jay Kim*, H. Rept. 105-797, 105th Cong., 2d Sess. 79 (1998) (noting the FBI provided "valuable assistance to the Investigative Subcommittee throughout its inquiry."); Comm. on Standards of Official Conduct, *Investigation Pursuant to House Resolution 12 Concerning Alleged Illicit Use or Distribution of Drugs by Members, Officers, or Employees of the House*, H. Rept. 98-559, 98th Cong., 1st Sess. 21 (1983) ("the Special Counsel and the Attorney General entered into an agreement whereby the Department was to provide the Committee non-privileged results of the Department's drug investigation, provided that access to the material was restricted to certain named individuals and that certain security precautions were taken."); Comm. on Standards of Official Conduct, *In the Matter of Representative Raymond F. Lederer*, H. Rept. 97-110, 97th Cong., 1st Sess. (1981); Comm. on Standards of Official Conduct, *In the Matter of Representative Michael J. Myers*, H. Rept. 96-1387, 96th Cong., 2d Sess. (1980); Comm. on Standards of Official Conduct, *In the Matter of Representative John W. Jenrette, Jr.*, H. Rept. 96-1537, 96th Cong., 2d Sess. 2 (1980) (noting the Special Counsel and DOJ entered into an agreement "covering the receipt of confidential information in respect to the investigation" into a Member who was a subject of DOJ investigations known as ABSCAM).

[9] Letter from U.S. Attorney's Office, U.S. Department of Justice, to Chairman Michael Guest and Ranking Member Susan Wild, Committee on Ethics (Feb. 13, 2024).

out particularized demands to the subpoena. Among the particularized demands was a request for any exculpatory evidence relating to Representative Gaetz. On March 13, 2024, Committee Members met with the Assistant Attorney General for the Office of Legislative Affairs and the Principal Deputy Assistant Attorney General for the Criminal Division of DOJ. The DOJ officials again cited no legal basis for failing to comply with the subpoena. DOJ subsequently requested additional context for the Committee's demands, which the Committee provided. After further attempts at meaningful accommodation of DOJ's concerns about the breadth of the Committee's request, DOJ ultimately provided publicly reported information about the testimony of a deceased individual. To date, DOJ has provided no meaningful evidence or information to the Committee or cited any lawful basis for its responses. The Committee hopes to continue to engage with DOJ on the broader issues raised by its failure to recognize the Committee's unique mandate. As the Committee has told DOJ, the Committee and DOJ should be partners in their shared mission of upholding the integrity of our government institutions.

The Committee initially made a narrowly tailored request for information to Representative Gaetz seeking information limited to the allegations that would not be within DOJ's jurisdiction—the alleged acceptance of an improper gift and sharing of nude images and videos on the House floor. The request also invited Representative Gaetz to provide additional information relevant to any of the allegations under review. Representative Gaetz sought numerous extensions and complained about the burden of the request. Representative Gaetz ultimately provided only three pages of information in response to the Committee's initial request.

On May 20, 2024, the Committee requested Representative Gaetz inform the Committee whether he would agree to participate in a voluntary interview and provided him a list of allegations so that he could make any response or provide any information regarding the allegations. On May 24, 2024, Representative Gaetz provided brief written denials of the allegations and "demand[ed] that the [C]ommittee address ['leaks'] prior to me providing any oral testimony to the Committee." On June 28, 2024, the Committee requested that Representative Gaetz provide the Committee with all records previously produced to DOJ, as well as dates of availability for an interview, by July 8. At that time, the Committee made an explicit request for any exonerating information.[10] The Committee also informed Representative Gaetz that it could not permit further delays. Representative Gaetz did not produce the requested documents or dates of availability, and on July 10, he asked for an extension through the August recess to produce documents he deemed "appropriate." Representative Gaetz did not provide these documents, despite multiple extensions provided by the Committee.

The Committee noted to Representative Gaetz that an interview would be an "opportunity to respond to the allegations against you and relevant questions arising out of the review."[11] However, he declined to voluntarily participate, again making demands of the Committee instead. On July 11, the Committee issued a subpoena for Representative Gaetz's testimony; the subpoena was served electronically to Representative Gaetz and his Chief of Staff, who had communicated

---

[10] *See, e.g.*, Letter from Representative Matt Gaetz to Chairman Michael Guest and Ranking Member Susan Wild, Committee on Ethics (June 24, 2024) ("It is highly likely that there is evidence which will exculpate me of any allegation that I have violated House Rules.").
[11] Letter from Chairman Michael Guest and Ranking Member Susan Wild, Committee on Ethics, to Representative Matt Gaetz (May 20, 2024).

with the Committee on behalf of the Congressman throughout the investigation. Representative Gaetz did not appear to testify pursuant to the Committee's subpoena. Representative Gaetz did not provide a legal basis for his failure to appear, but informed the Committee that, "[u]pon information and belief, the House will not take action to enforce" the subpoena. The Committee informed Representative Gaetz that, following his failure to comply with a subpoena and to provide a fulsome response to previous requests for information, the Committee would "rely on the record available to it to make its findings in this matter." Representative Gaetz responded by stating that he had prioritized providing evidence that "most clearly and directly proves [his] innocence," and stated that he "welcomed" written questions from the Committee. The Committee subsequently sent a set of written questions to Representative Gaetz. Representative Gaetz issued his response publicly, which did not answer most questions and asserted he would "no longer voluntarily participate" in the investigation.

On November 14, 2024, Representative Gaetz submitted his resignation to the House. On December 10, 2024, while several Members of the Committee objected, a majority of the Members voted to release the Report.

III. RELEVANT LAWS, RULES, AND OTHER APPLICABLE STANDARDS OF CONDUCT

A. Federal Laws

Section 1591 of Title 18, United States Code, prohibits trafficking (including recruiting, enticing, or transporting) a minor for commercial sex, while knowing or in reckless disregard of the fact that the victim is a minor.[12] Section 1591 also prohibits trafficking adults for commercial sex using "force, threats of force, fraud, or coercion."

The Mann Act, 18 U.S.C. § 2421 et seq., prohibits the knowing transportation of individuals through interstate or foreign commerce to engage in prostitution or other illegal sexual activity. Section 2423 specifically prohibits the transportation of minors with the intent to engage in commercial sex or illegal sexual activity. However, if a defendant establishes that (s)he "reasonably believed" that the individual with whom (s)he engaged in commercial sex was at least 18 years old, the defendant may avoid criminal liability. Sections 2421 and 2422 are not limited to transportation of minors, but the Criminal Division of DOJ has stated that it "does not prosecute these statutes in every case in which they are violated, but only where there is evidence of a victim of severe forms of trafficking in persons."[13]

Federal law also prohibits obstruction of Congress. Specifically, under 18 U.S.C. § 1505, it is a crime, either "corruptly"[14] or through threats, to influence, obstruct, or impede the "due and

---

[12] As defined in 18 U.S.C. § 1591(e)(3), commercial sex act "means any sex act, on account of which anything of value is given to or received by any person."
[13] *Statutes Enforced by the Criminal Section*, U.S. Department of Justice (last visited July 16, 2024), https://www.justice.gov/crt/statutes-enforced-criminal-section.
[14] 18 U.S.C. § 1515(b) ("As used in section 1505, the term 'corruptly' means acting with an improper purpose, personally or by influencing another, including making a false or misleading statement, or withholding, concealing, altering, or destroying a document or other information.").

proper exercise of the power of inquiry" of a House committee, or to endeavor to do so. Federal law also prohibits tampering with witnesses in a congressional proceeding; pursuant to 18 U.S.C. § 1512(b), it is a crime to knowingly intimidate, threaten or "corruptly persuade" (or attempt to do so), or to "engage[] in misleading conduct toward"[15] an individual with the intent to "influence, delay, or prevent the testimony of any person in an official proceeding," or to cause someone to withhold or alter evidence. The witness tampering statute also prohibits the lesser offense of intentionally harassing a witness in an attempt to dissuade the witness from testifying.[16] False statements to Congress in connection with an investigation are also prohibited, pursuant to 18 U.S.C. § 1001.

B. Florida State Laws

Under Florida's statutory rape law, it is a felony for a person 24 years of age or older to engage in sexual activity with a 16- or 17-year-old.[17] A person charged with this offense may not claim ignorance or misrepresentation of the minor's age as a defense.

It is also a criminal offense under Florida state law to solicit, induce, entice, or procure another to commit prostitution, or to "purchase the services of any person engaged in prostitution," or to "aid, abet, or participate" in such actions.[18] Florida defines prostitution as "the giving or receiving of the body for sexual activity for hire but excludes sexual activity between spouses."[19]

In Florida, unauthorized possession of controlled substances is also a criminal offense.[20] Schedule I and II controlled substances are deemed by Florida law as having a "high potential for abuse."[21] Cocaine and MDMA, commonly referred to as ecstasy or molly, are controlled substances under Florida law.[22]

C. House Rules and Other Standards of Conduct

Pursuant to 5 U.S.C. § 7353 and House Rule XXV, clause 5 (the Gift Rule), Members of Congress are subject to broad limitations on the solicitation and acceptance of gifts. Under the Gift Rule, Members may not knowingly accept any gift except as provided in the rule. As the *Ethics Manual* explains, gifts "include gratuities, favors, discounts, entertainment, hospitality, loans, forbearances, services, training, travel expenses, in-kind contributions, advanced payments, and reimbursements after the fact."[23] The general provision of the Gift Rule allows a Member to

---

[15] 18 U.S.C. § 1515(a)(3) (Misleading conduct is defined as knowingly making a false statement, intentionally omitting material information to create a false impression, inviting reliance on a writing or recording known to be inauthentic, and "knowingly using a trick, scheme, or device with intent to mislead.").
[16] 18 U.S.C. § 1512(d).
[17] FLA. STAT. § 794.05(1) (2023).
[18] FLA. STAT. §§ 796.07(2)(h), (i) (2023).
[19] FLA. STAT. § 796.07(1)(d) (2023).
[20] FLA. STAT. § 893.13(3)(e) (2023).
[21] FLA. STAT. §§ 893.03(1), (2) (2023).
[22] FLA. STAT. § 893.03(1) (2023).
[23] *House Ethics Manual* (2022) at 25 (hereinafter *Ethics Manual*); *see also* House Rule XXV, cl. 5(a)(2)(A).

accept a gift valued less than $50 so long as the source of the gift is not a registered lobbyist, foreign agent, or private entity that retains or employs such individuals.[24]

A gift received through a personal friendship where the fair market value is more than $250 requires formal approval from the Committee. With respect to a trip, the value is viewed as a whole and thus includes transportation, lodging, and meal expenses paid for by the gift-giver.[25] Certain considerations must be made in determining whether to accept a gift over $250 related to a personal friendship, such as (1) the history of the personal friendship, including any previous occasions of exchanging gifts; (2) whether the gift-giver personally paid for the gift or sought a tax deduction or business reimbursement for the gift; and (3) whether the gift-giver gave similar gifts to other Members, officers, or employees of the House.[26] In addition, Members are required to report the receipt of certain gifts from non-relatives where the aggregate value exceeds the "minimal value."[27] The minimum value in 2024 is $480 (excluding any gifts valued under $192); in 2018, it was $390 (excluding any gifts valued under $156).

There is also an exemption for gifts of personal hospitality, for which there is no value limit and no reporting requirement.[28] The personal hospitality exemption, however, is limited. It applies only to stays and meals in someone's personally-owned home, and it does not include air travel to get to that location or stays in a property that is rented out to others.

House Rule XXIII, clause 15, governs the payment for use of non-commercial aircraft by House Members. Members may use personal funds for the use of an aircraft supplied by an individual on the basis of personal friendship. Members may only accept a flight on a non-commercial aircraft without reimbursement under limited circumstances under the Gift Rule. As a general matter, the personal friendship exception can apply only if the aircraft is owned by the Member's personal friend, the use of the aircraft is for personal purposes, and the Member receives written approval from the Committee where the value is in excess of $250.

Section 5341 of Title 2, United States Code, establishing the Members' Representational Allowance, provides that its purpose is "to support the conduct of the official and representational duties of a Member [] with respect to the district from which the Member [] is elected." The *Ethics Manual* notes, however, that assistance to a non-constituent is not entirely prohibited under this statute and explains "[i]n some instances, working for non-constituents on matters that are similar to those facing constituents may enable the Member better to serve his or her district."[29] Nonetheless, Members "should not devote official resources to casework for individuals who live

---

[24] Caveats to this provision include: (1) the cumulative gift value from a single source in a calendar year must be less than $100; (2) a gift worth less than $10 does not count toward the cumulative limit; (3) cash or cash equivalents are not acceptable; and (4) buying down a gift value to less than the $50 limit is impermissible. *Ethics Manual* at 38; House Rule XXV, cl. 5(a)(1)(B)(i).
[25] *Ethics Manual* at 40.
[26] House Rule XXV, cl. 5(a)(3)(D)(ii); *see also Ethics Manual* at 41.
[27] *Ethics Manual* at 268 (also stating the minimal value is set by the General Services Administration every three years).
[28] House Rule XXV, cl. 5(a)(3)(P) (incorporating 5 U.S.C. app. § 109(14)).
[29] *Ethics Manual* at 317.

outside the district" but instead "may refer the person to his or her own Representative or Senator" for assistance.[30]

The Code of Ethics for Government Service sets forth standards of conduct for all government employees. Paragraph 2 of that Code provides that those in government service should "[u]phold the Constitution, laws, and legal regulations of the United States and of all governments therein and never be a party to their evasion." Paragraph 5 states that they should "[n]ever discriminate unfairly by the dispensing of special favors or privileges to anyone, whether for remuneration or not." All public servants are charged under the Code with upholding the principles articulated, "ever conscious that public office is a public trust."

House Rule XXIII, clause 1 states, "[a] Member . . . of the House shall behave at all times in a manner that shall reflect creditably on the House." House Rule XXIII, clause 2 states that Members "shall adhere to the spirit and the letter of the Rules of the House."

IV. FACTUAL BACKGROUND

A. Allegations of Sexual Misconduct and Drug Use

On March 30, 2021, the New York Times reported that Representative Gaetz was under investigation by DOJ for possible violation of sex trafficking laws.[31] The investigation reportedly related to allegations that Representative Gaetz had a sexual relationship with a 17-year-old and paid for her to travel with him. On April 1, 2021, additional reporting indicated the federal investigation included allegations involving cash payments, the use of illegal substances, the recruitment of women online for sex, and the use of campaign funds to pay for travel for women.[32] The DOJ investigation was part of an ongoing inquiry involving a former county tax collector in Florida named Joel Greenberg, who was sentenced to 11 years in prison in 2022.[33]

---

[30] *Id.*
[31] Michael S. Schmidt et al., *Matt Gaetz Is Said to Face Justice Dept. Inquiry Over Sex with an Underage Girl*, THE NEW YORK TIMES (Mar. 30, 2021), https://www.nytimes.com/2021/03/30/us/politics/matt-gaetz-sex-trafficking-investigation.html (hereinafter *Mar. 30 NYT Article*). Representative Gaetz voted against the Frederick Douglass Trafficking Victims Prevention & Protection Reauthorization Act of 2022 and was the lone "no" vote in 2017 on legislation to establish an advisory committee that would coordinate efforts to prevent human trafficking. In defending his 2017 vote, Representative Gaetz asserted that he worked in the Florida legislature to broaden the definition of "duress" in the state's trafficking law to include, *inter alia*, "economic duress." Matt Gaetz, FACEBOOK (Dec. 28, 2017), https://www.facebook.com/RepresentativeMattGaetz/videos/1498815083501178.
[32] Katie Benner and Michael S. Schmidt, *Justice Dept. Inquiry Into Matt Gaetz Said to Be Focused on Cash Paid to Women*, THE NEW YORK TIMES (Apr. 1, 2021), https://www.nytimes.com/2021/04/01/us/politics/matt-gaetz-justice-department.html (hereinafter *April 1 NYT Article*); Evan Perez et al., *Feds' Investigation of Matt Gaetz Includes Whether Campaign Funds Were Used to Pay for Travel and Expenses*, CNN (Apr. 1, 2021), https://www.cnn.com/2021/04/01/politics/matt-gaetz-campaign-funds-investigation/index.html.
[33] *See U.S. v. Joel Micah Greenberg*, No. 6:20-CR-97 (M.D. Fla. 2020) (Mr. Greenberg pleaded guilty to charges of sex trafficking of a minor, stalking, identity theft, wire fraud, and conspiracy to bribe a public official); *April 1 NYT Article*; Sara Dorn, *Former Matt Gaetz Associate Joel Greenberg Sentenced to 11 Years for Child Sex Trafficking*, FORBES (Dec. 1, 2022), https://www.forbes.com/sites/saradorn/2022/12/01/former-matt-gaetz-associate-joel-greenberg-sentenced-to-11-years-for-child-sex-trafficking/?sh=694d6c9e4dd3.

1. Representative Gaetz's Arrangement with Joel Greenberg

The Committee's record shows that, shortly after he was sworn into Congress in 2017, Representative Gaetz became friends with Mr. Greenberg, who had also recently taken office as the Seminole County tax collector. According to Mr. Greenberg, the two met at the house of Christopher Dorworth, a Florida lobbyist. Mr. Greenberg and Representative Gaetz frequently attended parties and other gatherings with young women in attendance. Many of those women were initially contacted by Mr. Greenberg via the website SeekingArrangement.com (now Seeking.com), and Mr. Greenberg subsequently introduced the women to Representative Gaetz. SeekingArrangement.com advertised itself as a "sugar dating" website that primarily connected older men and younger women seeking "mutually beneficial relationships."[34] The website was generally understood by many of the women interviewed by the Committee to involve, at minimum, an exchange of companionship for money.[35] There have been prosecutions against individuals for sex trafficking that originated with contacts made through SeekingArrangement.com or similar websites,[36] and some have called for the website to be shut down due to its facilitation of prostitution.[37] Platforms such as SeekingArrangement.com are known to "mak[e] it easier for traffickers to exploit victims and connect with buyers."[38]

---

[34] *See* Rebecca Downs, *Alternate to College Debt? Site Arranges Women to Use 'Sugar Daddies,'* THE WASHINGTON EXAMINER (May 19, 2016), https://washingtonexaminer.com/red-alert-politics/787936/alternate-to-college-debt-site-arranges-women-to-use-sugar-daddies.

[35] 18(a) Interview of Woman 5 ("[I]t was like a sugar daddy type website."); 18(a) Interview of Victim A ("I understood [the purpose of SeekingArrangement.com] to be meeting men to have sex or go on dates and get paid."); 18(a) Interview of Woman 6 (understanding the purpose of the website to be "[g]oing on dates with older men and getting paid for it."); 18(a) Interview of Woman 3 ("I understand it to be a sugar daddy website . . . . [I]t's pretty well known that that's what it is.").

[36] *E.g., Anton 'Tony' Lazzaro Sentenced to 21 Years in Prison for Child Sex Trafficking,* U.S. Attorney's Office, D. Minn. (Aug. 9, 2023), https://www.justice.gov/usao-mn/pr/anton-tony-lazzaro-sentenced-21-years-prison-child-sex-trafficking.

[37] *See Does Web Site Facilitate Prostitution? State Sen. Darren Soto Asks Florida's Attorney General to Shut Down Seekingarrangement.com,* NEWS4JAX (Feb. 14, 2013), https://www.news4jax.com/news/2013/02/14/does-web-site-facilitate-prostitution.

[38] *See* U.S. Government Accountability Office Report to Congressional Committees, *Sex Trafficking: Online Platforms and Federal Prosecutions* (June 2021), https://www.gao.gov/assets/gao-21-385.pdf. *See also* Jake Roberson, *The Dangers of Sugar Dating and Sugaring, Explained,* NATIONAL CENTER ON SEXUAL EXPLOITATION (Sept. 25, 2019), https://endsexualexploitation.org/articles/the-dangers-of-sugar-dating-and-sugaring-explained ("[T]he 'arrangements' are targeted toward—and often intentionally mislead—the younger, lower-income audience and puts them in situations where the natural end game is a variety of forms of manipulation and sexual exploitation"; "'Sugar dating' is not safe and it is not an empowering system—it is inherently exploitative."); Meeghan Sheppard, *Exposing the Exploitative Realities of Sugar Dating,* NATIONAL CENTER ON SEXUAL EXPLOITATION (July 2, 2020), https://endsexualexploitation.org/articles/exposing-the-exploitative-realities-of-sugar-dating ("For all intents and purposes, when the facade is stripped away, what is framed as a form of online dating meant to cultivate consenting relationships between two individuals is revealed as actually being a disturbing form of sexual exploitation."); Virginia Department of Criminal Justice Services, *An Introduction to Sex Trafficking: 2022 SRO Basic* (2022), https://www.dcjs.virginia.gov/sites/dcjs.virginia.gov/files/training-events/8020/introduction_to_sex_trafficking.pdf (noting that situations such as "arrangement dating" can "potentially escalate into [] human trafficking."); Laura E. Deeks, *A Website by Any Other Name? Sex, Sugar, and Section 230,* 34 Women's Rts. L. Rep. Law 245, 257 (2013) ("Under the banner of sugar daddy and sugar baby arrangements, a lot of prostitution may be going on.") (internal citations omitted); Melissa Farley et al., *Online*

The Committee did not receive any evidence that Representative Gaetz had his own account on SeekingArrangement.com. Mr. Greenberg indicated he frequently showed the site to Representative Gaetz and that he provided his login credentials to Representative Gaetz. According to Mr. Greenberg, he and Representative Gaetz would split the costs of "drugs, hotel[s], and girls." For example, the Committee reviewed evidence that such activity occurred in July 2017. Specifically, evidence showed that Representative Gaetz, Mr. Greenberg, and others gathered at a rental property located in the Brickell neighborhood of Miami, Florida for a weekend beginning on July 7, 2017; Representative Gaetz and Mr. Greenberg also spent time in Fort Lauderdale during the Miami stay (during which time Representative Gaetz withdrew at least $1,200 in cash from three different accounts at a single ATM). On June 22, 2017, Representative Gaetz paid $6,308 for that rental booking.[39] On July 9, 2017, Mr. Greenberg paid Representative Gaetz $1,600 by check; Mr. Greenberg stated the check was reimbursement for a share of the rental.[40] Mr. Greenberg also noted that they met up with another individual for dinner that weekend, and he shared a photo of Representative Gaetz, himself, and the other individual on social media on July 8, 2017.[41]

The Committee received evidence confirming that Representative Gaetz at times personally made payments to women who attended parties with him and Mr. Greenberg, using various peer-to-peer electronic payment services, as well as checks and cash. The Committee's record also indicates that Mr. Greenberg sometimes paid women for having sex with Representative Gaetz and was sometimes reimbursed by Representative Gaetz.[42] Witnesses indicated that there were times where a lump sum would be sent to one woman, who would then distribute the money evenly among others who attended the parties. Likewise, in one instance

---

Prostitution and Trafficking, 77 Albany L. Rev. 1039, 1056 (2014) ("Compartmentalization of the sex industry into illegal versus quasi-legal prostitution [referencing seekingarrangement.com] benefits pimps and traffickers in that it frequently avoids accountability for criminal acts."); Jacqueline Motyl, *Trading Sex for College Tuition: How Sugar Daddy "Dating" Sites May Be Sugar Coating Prostitution*, 117:3 Dickinson L. Rev. 927. 956-57 (2013) ("[S]ugar daddy dating sites may not be the most pressing issue regarding prostitution, but enough is known to suggest and perhaps predict that increasingly questionable individuals and activities may migrate to these sites" allowing for "prostitution-type arrangements to foster within the Sugar Culture.").

[39] Personal Checking Account #3. Records obtained by the Committee show that this vacation rental was booked via an account belonging to one of Representative Gaetz's former congressional staffers and paid for via Personal Checking Account #3.

[40] Exhibit 1. Mr. Greenberg claimed that he and Representative Gaetz did drugs the entire weekend. Venmo records show that Mr. Greenberg paid several hundred dollars to two of the women he identified as present for the weekend, with a note that the payment was for "food." One of the women identified by Mr. Greenberg asserted her Fifth Amendment privilege when asked questions about the purpose of the payments from Mr. Greenberg, including whether any of the payments were for drugs.

[41] Joel Greenberg (@JoelGreenbergTC), X (formerly Twitter) (July 8, 2017, 10:00 PM), https://x.com/JoelGreenbergTC/status/883868335955480576.

[42] For example, the Committee reviewed a contemporaneous text message showing that one of the women with whom both Representative Gaetz and Mr. Greenberg engaged in sexual activity contacted Mr. Greenberg to complain about not receiving expected money from him; Mr. Greenberg responded at the time indicating that he was waiting on money from Representative Gaetz. Exhibit 2 (Woman 4 testified that she saved Representative Gaetz on her phone as "Marissa" for discretion. (18(a) Interview of Woman 4.)). Financial records reviewed by the Committee generally corroborate Mr. Greenberg's assertions that Representative Gaetz would sometimes send him money to cover his portion of payments owed to women.

Representative Gaetz sent $400 to Mr. Greenberg with the note "Hit up [Victim A]"; Mr. Greenberg then sent two women payments totaling $400, including Victim A.[43]

On August 19, 2020, Mr. Greenberg was indicted on charges related to his misuse of motor vehicle records and identification documents in his role as Seminole County tax collector and his attempt to falsely accuse a political opponent of being a pedophile; he was additionally charged with sex trafficking of a child (Victim A), wire fraud, bribery of a public official, theft of government property, and related charges. He pleaded guilty to six charges, including sex trafficking of Victim A, in May 2021 but his sentencing was delayed until December 2022 due to his ongoing cooperation in several other matters. As part of his cooperation, he provided information that was ultimately corroborated and ended in successful prosecutions.[44]

2. Representative Gaetz's Interactions with Women He Met Through Mr. Greenberg

   i. Transactional Nature of the Interactions

From 2017 to 2020, Representative Gaetz made tens of thousands of dollars in payments to women that the Committee determined were likely in connection with sexual activity and/or drug use.[45] Payments were made to these women using peer-to-peer payment platforms such as PayPal, Venmo, and CashApp; while Representative Gaetz had accounts in his name on each of those platforms, he also sometimes paid women through another person's PayPal account, or through an account held under a pseudonymous e-mail account.[46] Representative Gaetz also paid

---

[43] Personal Venmo Account #1; Mr. Greenberg Venmo Account #1. Representative Gaetz's initial attempt to send the payment did not go through; in that attempt, the note stated, "Don't forget to hit [Victim A] up. She was on me."
[44] Nonetheless, as the Committee has acknowledged, there are concerns regarding Mr. Greenberg's credibility. Representative Gaetz was also aware that Mr. Greenberg was not an entirely trustworthy individual: "We all joked about how Joel is going to get us in trouble one day"; Representative Gaetz was "aware" that it was not smart to "be hanging out with [Joel] because he wasn't a very [up]standing person" (18(a) Interview of Woman 5); Mr. Greenberg's personality was "not one that really lends to what you would call a traditional, conventional friend"; Mr. Greenberg "exists in a manic[] state"; "Congressman Gaetz and I had many conversations about concerns about what kind of guy Joel Greenberg was"; and Mr. Greenberg would "walk[] around with a bunch of young women he met online and things like that" (18(a) Interview of Christopher Dorworth).
[45] The Committee determined that a small portion of the payments was for drugs. See Exhibit 3.
[46] Personal Venmo Account #1; Personal CashApp Account #1; Affiliated PayPal Account #1; Affiliated PayPal Account #2. The pseudonymous e-mail account was subject to a user-initiated deletion in September 2017 and purged of all records including emails, photographs, and calendars, as well as access to certain applications, subscriptions, and content. Google only maintains deleted accounts for short periods in case a user wishes to recover it. See Google Account Help, Delete Your Google Account or Google Services https://support.google.com/accounts/answer/32046?hl=en; Google Account Help, Recover a Recently Deleted Google Account, https://support.google.com/accounts/answer/6236295?sjid=7679482182268347965-NA. Representative Gaetz appears to have initially set up the pseudonymous e-mail account in order to make payments relating to cannabis products, and then also used it to make payments to women. The witnesses interviewed by the Committee consistently testified that Representative Gaetz was a frequent user of marijuana. See, e.g., 18(a) Interview of Woman 5 ("I provided him some cartridges...[o]f marijuana."); 18(a) Interview of Woman 3 ("I know [Representative Gaetz] had his weed pen on him a lot of the times."); 18(a) Interview of Woman 7 ("I've seen him smoking marijuana.").

some of the women by check or in cash.[47]

The following chart summarizes payments made by Representative Gaetz to Mr. Greenberg and to women via peer-to-peer payment platforms or checks:

Recipient	Amount[48]	Timeframe
Woman 1[49] (former girlfriend)	$63,836.58	2017-2020
Woman 2	$4,189.82	2019-2020
Woman 3	$2,651.69	2018-2019
Woman 4	$6,198.75	2017-2019
Woman 5	$4,025.27	2018-2019
Woman 6	$5,251.23	2018-2019
Woman 7	$200.00	2018
Woman 8	$600.00	2017
Woman 9	$1,280.00	2018-2020
Woman 10	$400.00	2018
Woman 11	$500.00	2017
Woman 12	$2,135.48	2018-2019
Joel Greenberg	$3,950.00	2018-2019

The Committee's record indicates that Representative Gaetz was in a long-term relationship with Woman 1, and therefore some of the payments may have been of a legitimate nature; however, as discussed further below, Woman 1 asserted her Fifth Amendment right when asked whether the payments to her from Representative Gaetz were for sexual activity and/or drugs, or for her to pass on to others for such purposes. Based on that assertion combined with evidence received from other sources, the Committee found substantial reason to believe that most of these payments were for such activity.

The Committee was not able to speak with every woman who received payments from Representative Gaetz that were suspected of being part of illicit activity. Several women initially were responsive to the Committee's outreach but later told the Committee they would not voluntarily participate. Other women were clear at first contact that they feared retaliation or were unwilling to voluntarily relive their interactions with Representative Gaetz. Due to the women's reluctance to cooperate, as well as the delay caused by DOJ's deferral request and subsequent refusal to provide meaningful cooperation, the Committee was unable to determine the full extent to which Representative Gaetz's payments to women were compensation for engaging in sexual activity with him. However, the record before the Committee provides substantial reason to

---

[47] One male witness recalled seeing Representative Gaetz give cash to a woman at a party at his home. He asked Representative Gaetz whether the payment was for sex, which Representative Gaetz denied. When asked whether he believed Representative Gaetz, the witness stated only that he "wanted to believe" him. 18(a) Interview of Individual 1. Mr. Greenberg also received cash reimbursements for paying women on Representative Gaetz's behalf.
[48] Amount does not include cash or checks to cash that may have ultimately been received by the women; it also does not include amounts paid by other individuals to women on behalf of Representative Gaetz.
[49] Amount does not include payments of attorney's fees.

believe that many of the payments in the chart above were made in connection with sexual activity and/or illicit drug use. The Committee was also not able to quantify the amount of cash payments Representative Gaetz made to women,[50] or the amount of payments that other individuals, such as Mr. Greenberg, made on behalf of Representative Gaetz.

Representative Gaetz refused to answer questions about his relationships with the women involved. There was, however, evidence that he understood and shared many of the women's transactional views of their arrangements. In one text exchange viewed by the Committee, Representative Gaetz balked at a woman's request that he send her money after he accused her of "ditching" him on a night when she was feeling tired, claiming she only gave him a "drive by." The woman asserted to Representative Gaetz that she was being "treated differently" than other women he was paying for sex.[51] The Committee also obtained text messages in which Representative Gaetz's then-girlfriend informed some of the women who were typically paid for sex that "the guys [Representative Gaetz and Mr. Greenberg] wanted me to share that they are a little limited in their cash flow this weekend . . . [M]att was like[,] if it can be more of a customer appreciation week. . . ."[52] A few months later, she noted that, "Btw Matt also mentioned he is going to be a bit generous cause of the 'customer appreciation' thing last time." Another woman specifically recalled a conversation with Representative Gaetz about issues with Mr. Greenberg's "following through" with expected payments after Mr. Greenberg's encounters with her.[53] Mr. Greenberg told the Committee that Representative Gaetz was aware that the women they had sex with and paid had met Mr. Greenberg through the "sugar dating" website.

Representative Gaetz did not appear to have negotiated specific payment amounts prior to engaging in sexual activity with the women he paid. Instead, the women had a general expectation that they would typically receive some amount of money after each sexual encounter. In 2017, using a pseudonymous account, Representative Gaetz made payments to women largely without a description of the purpose of the payment. After several months, he began to use other payment accounts, including ones with his own name, using innocuous descriptions to indicate the purpose of the payments.[54] Representative Gaetz did not provide any information regarding the tens of thousands of dollars in payments he made to over a dozen women despite being offered the opportunity to do so by the Committee. Representative Gaetz was provided with a list of women who the Committee found received payments from him beginning in 2017 and was asked to inform the Committee of the purpose of those payments, as well as to inform the Committee how he knew

---

[50] Representative Gaetz withdrew more than $25,000 in cash from 2017-2018 alone. *See* Personal Checking Account #2; Personal Checking Account #3; Personal Checking Account #4.

[51] Some women appeared mindful of their own potential liability and were reluctant to acknowledge explicit discussions of sex-for-hire. The Committee received some testimony indicating that there may have at times been miscommunications about the transactional nature of their interactions, but that it was ultimately made clear. One woman testified, "[m]aybe I was under the impression that Joel [Greenberg] had talked to [Representative Gaetz] about kind of what was supposed to happen. I think maybe [Representative Gaetz] even didn't really understand at some points because maybe that's why he wasn't giving me what I wanted. So I think there was definitely some miscommunication, and then maybe Joel promised stuff, and he wasn't keeping it. I don't really know what was going on behind the scenes with them or that kind of stuff. But I would assume that he understood, considering he did send me money at one point." 18(a) Interview of Woman 4.

[52] Exhibit 4.

[53] 18(a) Interview of Woman 5.

[54] *See* Exhibit 3.

the individual and whether, "*if* you engaged in any sexual activity with the individual, did she ever indicate to you that she expected payment for engaging in sexual activity with you?"[55] Rather than answer the questions, Representative Gaetz asserted incorrectly: "You ask, in part, whether I've had sex with a list of adult women over the past seven years. The lawful, consensual, sexual activities of adults are not the business of Congress."

Many of the women interviewed by the Committee were clear that there was a general expectation of sex. One woman who was paid more than $5,000 by Representative Gaetz between 2018 and 2019 told the Committee that "99 percent of the time that [Representative Gaetz and I] were hanging out, there was sex involved."[56]

Text messages obtained by the Committee show that Representative Gaetz would also ask women to bring drugs to their rendezvous, in some instances requesting marijuana cartridges and repaying the women directly, but in other cases requesting "a full compliment [sic] of party favors," "vitamins," or "rolls."[57] Representative Gaetz sent one woman several hundred dollars for marijuana cartridges.[58] One woman stated that, with respect to a 2018 Bahamas trip, "[M]yself and [Representative Gaetz's then-girlfriend] brought drugs with us, and I do know that Matt supplied [his then-girlfriend] with money."[59] Another woman said that she brought cocaine to at least one event with Representative Gaetz and that she witnessed him taking cocaine or ecstasy on at least five occasions.[60] Mr. Greenberg told the Committee that he would typically provide drugs, such as ecstasy, for events he attended and Representative Gaetz would pay him back in cash. Several other women observed Representative Gaetz to be under the influence of drugs.[61] Additionally, nearly every witness interviewed observed Representative Gaetz using marijuana.[62]

ii. Selected Interactions

Based on the evidentiary record, the Committee identified at least 20 occasions from the beginning of 2017 through the middle of 2020 where there was substantial evidence that Representative Gaetz met with women who were paid for sex and/or drugs. The Committee also received testimony related to multiple additional events, trips, or parties where Representative

---

[55] *See* Appendix A (emphasis added).
[56] *Id. See also* 18(a) Interview of Woman 13 ("Matt Gaetz paid me for sex, that was the extent of our interaction."); 18(a) Interview of Woman 5 ("it was understood . . . that [sex for money] was the arrangement.").
[57] Exhibit 4; Exhibit 5. Woman 5 explained that "rolls" referred to ecstasy. *See also Slang Terms and Code Words: A Reference for Law Enforcement Personnel*, Drug Enforcement Administration (July 2018), https://www.dea.gov/sites/default/files/2018-07/DIR-022-18.pdf (listing "vitamin E" and "rolls" as slang for ecstasy/MDMA/molly). The Committee was not able to determine how and when Representative Gaetz paid for "party favors" such as ecstasy and cocaine.
[58] *See* Personal Venmo Account #1; 18(a) Interview of Woman 5.
[59] 18(a) Interview of Woman 5 (also noting that she (Woman 5), Representative Gaetz's then-girlfriend (Woman 1), or Mr. Greenberg would typically supply drugs).
[60] 18(a) Interview of Woman 6.
[61] *See, e.g.*, 18(a) Interview of Woman 4 (stating, for example, on one occasion Representative Gaetz was "talkative, sexual[] . . . he stayed up late, like probably the whole night with everybody" and that the "appearance of his face, eyes" were indicators of his having taken ecstasy); 18(a) Interview of Woman 5 (stating that on a different occasions Representative Gaetz "exhibited signs of being on ecstasy").
[62] *See, e.g.*, 18(a) Interview of Woman 3; 18(a) Interview of Woman 4; 18(a) Interview of Woman 5; 18(a) Interview of Woman 7; 18(a) Interview of Individual 1; 18(a) Interview of Christopher Dorworth.

Gaetz may have paid women for sex and drugs, although the Committee could not determine the specific dates or locations for all of them. To the extent Representative Gaetz paid money to women in connection with those trips, at least some such transactions are reflected in the chart discussed in the prior section.

One of the women that Mr. Greenberg met on SeekingArrangement.com and introduced to Representative Gaetz in or around March 2017 became Representative Gaetz's girlfriend, when he was almost 35 and she was 21 years old; their relationship continued for over two years. The relationship was not exclusive, and the Committee received evidence that Representative Gaetz's then-girlfriend sometimes participated with him in sexual encounters with other women who were active on the website or otherwise involved in sex-for-money arrangements. The Committee also obtained text messages where she appeared to act as an intermediary between Representative Gaetz and the women he paid for sex. She herself was paid tens of thousands of dollars by Representative Gaetz over the course of their two-year relationship; she stated "Matt always paid for anything for me."[63] However, she invoked her Fifth Amendment right against self-incrimination in response to several questions, including what the purpose of specific payments was, whether Representative Gaetz ever paid her money for sex, and whether she was aware of Representative Gaetz paying others for sex. She also invoked her Fifth Amendment privilege when asked to explain an increase in payments from Representative Gaetz in 2019, whether any of the payments from Representative Gaetz were related to drugs, and whether payments she received from Mr. Greenberg were related to Representative Gaetz.

The Committee obtained messages between Mr. Greenberg and a 20-year-old woman he met through SeekingArrangement.com who noted, "I usually do $400 per meet." As shown in the following exchange, Mr. Greenberg and the woman made plans to each bring a friend to their meet. The Committee found that the language used by the woman and amount proposed were consistent with typical "pay per meet" arrangements made by users of SeekingArrangement.com at that time.[64]

---

[63] 18(a) Interview of Woman 1. This amount does not include the $50,025 Representative Gaetz paid her attorneys at the outset of DOJ's investigation. His then-girlfriend indicated he paid for her attorneys "because he cares for me, wants me to be protected and safe." *Id.* Other witnesses indicated that they understood Representative Gaetz to have a financial relationship with his then-girlfriend.

[64] *See, e.g.*, Lauren Seabrook, *UCF Sugar Babies Talk Sugar Daddy Foot Fetish, Arrangements Netting Up to $500 a Date*, WFTV9 (Apr. 26, 2019), https://www.wftv.com/news/9-investigates/ucf-sugar-babies-explain-arrangements-that-net-up-to-500-a-date-talk-sugar-daddy-foot-fetish/943137086; Anonymous, *I'm a 'Sugar Baby' Who Gets Paid $500 a Date – Here's What It's Really Like to Date Sugar Daddies and Get Cash, Gifts, and 5-Star Hotel Stays*, BUSINESS INSIDER (Aug. 8, 2022), https://www.businessinsider.com/sugar-baby-relationship-sugar-daddy-what-its-like-2019-8; REDDIT (r/sugarlifestyleforum), https://www.reddit.com/r/sugarlifestyleforum.

> **Messages between Joel Greenberg and 20 year-old Female**
>
> If you have a friend that is down, perhaps all four of us can meet up later.
>
> Do you party at all?
>
> Sep 22, 2018
>
> Oh that's perfect. I have a friend who introduced me to the website that I could bring. She's very pretty, great personality. I usually do $400 per meet, does your friend use the website as well? And yes I do like to go out sometimes 😊
>
> ▬▬▬(iPhone) · Sep 22, 2018
>
> Very cool. Yes he understands the deal :)
>
> What does your friend look like?
>
> $400 is not a problem. Are you both old enough to drink ?
>
> Sep 22, 2018

> So what do you have in mind for tonight?
>
> ▬▬▬Phone) · Sep 22, 2018
>
> My friend
>
> Sep 22, 2018
>
> Oooh my friend thinks he's really cute!
>
> ▬▬▬(iPhone) · Sep 22, 2018
>
> Well, he's down here only for the day, we work hard and play hard.
>
> Have you ever tried molly
>
> Sep 22, 2018

[65]

Evidence reviewed by the Committee shows that, on several occasions, Representative Gaetz met with the woman who corresponded with Mr. Greenberg in these messages; he continues to follow her on social media and has paid her more than $2,000 since late 2018.

The Committee received evidence indicating that the 20-year-old woman in the above messages joined Mr. Greenberg and Representative Gaetz at a hotel in Florida less than two weeks after her initial encounter with Representative Gaetz. The Committee's record indicates that Representative Gaetz also invited another woman who he regularly paid for sex to meet him at the hotel, without disclosing to her that others would be present. The other woman, who was 21 years old, had recently asked the congressman for his help with her tuition. She recalled that Representative Gaetz agreed and told her to meet him at that hotel room, where he would provide her with a check, which, according to the woman, "was interesting because he had normally sent Venmo payments."[66] When she arrived to pick up the check, she found Mr. Greenberg and the 20-year-old woman present. The 21-year-old woman told the Committee there was an "expectation" of a "sexual encounter." The four of them had sex and afterwards Representative Gaetz gave her a $750 check made out to cash with "tuition reimbursement" in the memo line, which she deposited the next day to help pay her tuition.[67] The 21-year-old woman told the Committee she believed that the encounter "could potentially be a form of coercion because I

---

[65] Image has been altered to redact a woman's name and images of minors.
[66] 18(a) Interview of Woman 5.
[67] Personal Checking Account #4.

really needed the money."⁶⁸ Representative Gaetz's financial records confirm that he wrote the check, and that he was present at the hotel identified by the woman, on the date identified by the woman.⁶⁹

As another example, the Committee obtained text messages that appeared to show Representative Gaetz messaging a woman he knew through Mr. Greenberg, inviting her to travel on a private plane to Key West from May 19-21, 2017, with "2 guys, 4 girls. A very high-quality, adventurous group."⁷⁰ She initially responded, "Yeah I'm in," to which Representative Gaetz stated, "Fantastic. As is true with all time you spend w[ith] me, it'll be fun and very chill." The same woman was photographed with Representative Gaetz on May 19, 2017, in Orlando. The photograph depicts Representative Gaetz in a casual shirt with his arm around her in a dimly lit bar. She was also photographed in front of a helicopter with three other women associated with Representative Gaetz around the same time, including his then-girlfriend. After the Committee obtained copies of the text messages and "selfie" photo, there was public reporting about the evidence.⁷¹ In response to the reporting, Representative Gaetz's spokesperson released a statement asserting that "Rep. Gaetz does not know anything about the woman you're referencing, though he takes thousands of selfies each year."⁷² Payment records reviewed by the Committee, however, show that Representative Gaetz paid $600 to the woman the same day he was photographed with her.

In February 2018, Mr. Greenberg introduced Representative Gaetz to two women with accounts on SeekingArrangement.com. They were generally older than the other women that Mr. Greenberg had previously introduced to Representative Gaetz, and they had a slightly different relationship with the two men. They were the only women paid by Representative Gaetz who denied to the Committee that the payments they received from the congressman were compensation for engaging in sexual activity.

One of the women, who was 25 years old when she met Representative Gaetz, testified that she understood herself to be more "sophisticated" than some other women on SeekingArrangement.com. In contrast to the women who almost exclusively interacted with Representative Gaetz in hotel rooms or at private parties,⁷³ this woman attended events as

---

⁶⁸ 18(a) Interview of Woman 5. Contemporaneous messages reviewed by the Committee show that Representative Gaetz also understood the urgency of the woman's need to pay for classes on a deadline.
⁶⁹ Personal Checking Account #2; Personal Checking Account #4.
⁷⁰ Exhibit 6.
⁷¹ *See* Will Steakin, *House Panel Obtains Texts Allegedly Showing Gaetz Setting Up 2017 Florida Keys Trip with Woman His Associate Paid for Sex: Sources*, ABC NEWS (Feb. 14, 2024), https://abcnews.go.com/US/house-panel-obtains-texts-allegedly-showing-gaetz-setting/story?id=107126493 (hereinafter *February 14 ABC Article*). Representative Gaetz repeatedly accused the Committee of being responsible for "leaking" this information to the press. The Committee was not responsible for the disclosure of evidence. The same records were in the possession of multiple individuals at the time of the disclosure due to the civil litigation relating to the allegations against Representative Gaetz.
⁷² *Id.*
⁷³ The Committee received evidence that Representative Gaetz invited some of the younger women to hotels where political events were occurring. Representative Gaetz advised the women on what to wear when attending such events. *See* Exhibit 5 (Rep. Gaetz: "let's talk wardrobe … [d]o you have a cute black dress? … Can't be toooo short. But sexy def OK.").

Representative Gaetz's date, for which she was paid between $500 and $1,000 per event.[74] She also stated that she did not feel pressured to have sex with Representative Gaetz, and only did so on some occasions.[75] She told the Committee that, in December 2019, Representative Gaetz had his congressional assistant arrange travel for her to Washington, D.C. for one night.[76] According to the woman, she attended a dinner with Representative Gaetz and a few other individuals.[77] She stayed overnight at a hotel with Representative Gaetz and had sex with him. Representative Gaetz sent the woman $1,000 around that time. The woman told the Committee she was paid to be his date and that sex was not necessarily an expectation.[78]

The other older woman, who was 27 years old when she met Representative Gaetz, was the only woman interviewed by the Committee who did not view their relationship as transactional in nature.[79] The first time she met Representative Gaetz, however, she had sex with him and was paid $1,000 by Mr. Greenberg, which she understood to have been at Representative Gaetz's direction. She told the Committee that she viewed her relationship with Representative Gaetz as "more or less" dating, although "it was never anything serious."[80] She said she was not familiar with his then-girlfriend, and said she was not aware that he was also having a sexual relationship with her friend, the 25-year-old woman. She frequently commented on his social media, and he still follows her on social media.

Most of the sex-for-money encounters that the Committee reviewed occurred in Florida, particularly around Orlando. Several of the women involved were students based in that area. On several occasions, however, Representative Gaetz did travel with women that he paid for sex.

On September 13, 2018, Representative Gaetz, two other men, and six women traveled to the Bahamas. Representative Gaetz arrived by commercial plane later than the others, who arrived on private planes. The group stayed at a vacation rental booked and paid for by one of the male travelers.[81] The attendees stated that this was a social trip—they sunbathed, chartered a boat, and went to dinners and to a casino as a group. Representative Gaetz engaged in sexual activity with at least four of the women on the trip.[82] Several of the women recalled that Representative Gaetz

---

[74] 18(a) Interview of Woman 6 (stating that the money was "pretty much to stand there, take pictures, and smile.").
[75] *Id.*
[76] Personal CashApp Account #1.
[77] Representative Gaetz referenced this dinner in a March 30, 2021 media interview: "[Y]ou and I went to dinner about two years ago, your wife was there, and I brought a friend of mine, you'll remember her . . . ." Teo Armus, *Tucker Carlson Denies Gaetz Claim That He Met Witness in FBI Probes: 'One of the Weirdest Interviews I've Ever Conducted*, THE WASHINGTON POST (Mar. 31, 2021) (hereinafter *Carlson Interview*), https://www.washingtonpost.com/nation/2021/03/31/tucker-carlson-matt-gaetz-17.
[78] 18(a) Interview of Woman 6.
[79] As one example, the Committee asked this woman about a $550 payment she received from Representative Gaetz in 2018, which occurred around the same time she attended an event with Representative Gaetz and had sex with him. The woman told the Committee that the $550 payment was reimbursement for a dress she purchased to wear to the event. 18(a) Interview of Woman 3.
[80] *Id.*
[81] Exhibit 7.
[82] 18(a) Interview of Woman 1 (stating that she was a "witness" to Representative Gaetz engaging in sexual activity with other women on the trip); 18(a) Interview of Woman 4 ("I had sex with [Representative Gaetz] at the Airbnb that we were staying in in the Bahamas." However, in the civil litigation, Woman 4 stated that she did not

appeared to be under the influence of drugs and that they took ecstasy during this trip; one woman said she witnessed Representative Gaetz taking ecstasy as well.[83] Most, if not all, of the women involved had some history of sexual interactions with Representative Gaetz for which they had been paid. While there were no specific payments to the women in connection with the Bahamas trip, according to one woman, "the trip itself was more so the payment."[84] The group returned to Orlando on September 16, 2018; Representative Gaetz flew on a private plane with another man and three women, while the remaining individuals flew on another private plane.

Representative Gaetz paid for two women to travel to New York City in January 2019 to meet up with him and his then-girlfriend. The Committee reviewed text messages in which Representative Gaetz asked the women about obtaining drugs in advance of the trip, stating, "[w]ho can help w[ith] party favors?"[85] In addition to paying for their travel costs, the Committee received evidence that Representative Gaetz sent the women money to compensate them for sexual activities they engaged in with him during the trip.[86]

While all the women that the Committee interviewed stated their sexual activity with Representative Gaetz was consensual, at least one woman felt that the use of drugs at the parties and events they attended may have "impair[ed their] ability to really know what was going on or fully consent."[87] Indeed, nearly every woman that the Committee spoke with could not remember the details of at least one or more of the events they attended with Representative Gaetz and attributed that to drug or alcohol consumption.[88] The women also discussed instances where Representative Gaetz would try to convince them to have sex with him or Mr. Greenberg: "[H]e would make me feel bad about not having sex with him or [] Joel Greenberg" and that he would say, "Why don't you want to have sex with me" or "[Mr. Greenberg] looks very sad over there . . . . Make him happy."[89] Another woman said that their relationship at some point was a "loving friendship," but over time came to feel like a "task."[90] A third woman said, "[W]hen I look back on certain moments, I feel violated."[91] One woman said, "I think about it all the time . . . . I still see him when I turn on the tv and there's nothing anyone can do. It's frustrating to know I lived a reality that he denies."[92]

---

participate in sexual activity in the Bahamas.); 18(a) Interview of Victim A ("I joined in . . . when[] [Representative Gaetz] was with all of those women in the bedroom.").

[83] 18(a) Interview of Victim A.
[84] 18(a) Interview of Woman 5.
[85] Exhibit 8.
[86] *Id.*; *see also* Exhibit 3; 18(a) Interview of Woman 5.
[87] 18(a) Interview of Woman 4.
[88] *Id.*; 18(a) Interview of Victim A; 18(a) Interview of Woman 1; 18(a) Interview of Woman 5.
[89] 18(a) Interview of Victim A.
[90] 18(a) Interview of Woman 5.
[91] 18(a) Interview of Victim A (also commenting that she "thought all of those people were my friends . . . . I know now that [] they're not.").
[92] 18(a) Interview of Woman 13.

3. Representative Gaetz's Interactions with the Minor He Met Through Mr. Greenberg

Numerous witnesses told the Committee that, on July 15, 2017, Representative Gaetz attended a party at Mr. Dorworth's home.[93] This party was also attended by Mr. Greenberg, Representative Gaetz's then-girlfriend, and several others, including Victim A, who was 17 years old at the time. The record overwhelmingly suggests that Representative Gaetz had sex with multiple women at the party, including the then-17-year-old, for which they were paid.[94]

Mr. Dorworth testified that Representative Gaetz was a frequent guest at his home.[95] To enter the community where Mr. Dorworth lives, non-residents are required to present a driver's license before entering, and entry records are maintained.[96] Mr. Dorworth believed that Representative Gaetz invited people to his home on the evening of July 15, 2017.[97] Likewise, Representative Gaetz's then-girlfriend provided an affidavit in the civil litigation stating that she and Representative Gaetz attended the July 15, 2017, party at the Dorworth residence.[98]

The Committee received testimony that Victim A and Representative Gaetz had sex twice during the party, including at least once in the presence of other party attendees.[99] Victim A recalled receiving $400 in cash from Representative Gaetz that evening, which she understood to be payment for sex.[100] At the time, she had just completed her junior year of high school.[101] Victim A said that she did not inform Representative Gaetz that she was under 18 at the time, nor

---

[93] *Id.*; 18(a) Interview of Woman 4; 18(a) Interview of Victim A; Sworn response of Joel Greenberg.; *see also* Exhibit 9 (showing that Woman 1, Victim A, and Woman 4 were present at the party).
[94] 18(a) Interview of Victim A; 18(a) Interview of Woman 1; 18(a) Interview of Woman 4. Mr. Greenberg informed the Committee that the day after this party, Representative Gaetz bragged that "he had sex with six girls in one day and named all of them," including Victim A.
[95] 18(a) Interview of Christopher Dorworth (stating that Representative Gaetz would stay at his home three to five times a year, and that his home has seven bedrooms).
[96] The records only list the vehicle and driver; it does not include passengers.
[97] *See* Exhibit 9 (showing at least five individuals arriving between 3:20 p.m. and 11:16 p.m.). Mr. Dorworth's wife testified in the civil litigation that she also thought Representative Gaetz was at her home on July 15, 2017, and another individual testified in that litigation that Representative Gaetz was at Mr. Dorworth's house when he arrived that evening. One woman provided an affidavit in the civil litigation stating that, "Over the course of the Summer and into the Fall of 2017, I attended gatherings at the Dorworth Residence with alcohol; cocaine; middle-aged men; and young, attractive females."
[98] Woman 4 also provided an affidavit in the civil litigation placing Representative Gaetz at Mr. Dorworth's house during the July 15, 2017, party.
[99] Although one witness indicated that Representative Gaetz and Victim A had sex with Representative Gaetz's then-girlfriend present and participating, another witness indicated that Representative Gaetz's then-girlfriend did not have sex with Victim A at that specific party. One individual stated she saw Representative Gaetz and Victim A having sex; her testimony was consistent to both the Committee and in the civil litigation. The Committee also received evidence that Mr. Dorworth may have observed Representative Gaetz and Victim A having sex at the party; Victim A said he walked in on her and Representative Gaetz having sex and that Mr. Dorworth was "joking about it with other people at the party." 18(a) Interview of Victim A. Mr. Dorworth testified that he was not home that evening. 18(a) Interview of Christopher Dorworth. However, phone records for Mr. Dorworth indicate that he was home at approximately 7:00 p.m. and did not leave until the following day. Additionally, multiple individuals provided testimony and affidavits in the civil litigation asserting Mr. Dorworth was home on the evening of July 15.
[100] In the week leading up to this party, Representative Gaetz withdrew at least $1,200 cash over three transactions. *See* Personal Checking Account #2; Personal Checking Account #3; Personal Checking Account #4.
[101] Victim A did not turn 18 until later in 2017.

did he ask her age. The Committee did not receive any evidence indicating that Representative Gaetz was aware that Victim A was a minor when he had sex with her.

Victim A acknowledged that she was under the influence of ecstasy during her sexual encounters with Representative Gaetz at the July 15, 2017, party, and recalled seeing Representative Gaetz use cocaine at that party.[102] Victim A told the Committee she was "certain" of her sexual encounters with Representative Gaetz on that night.[103] As discussed further below, Representative Gaetz generally denied engaging in sexual activity with a minor but refused to answer specific questions relating to his interactions with Victim A.

On August 2, 2024, Representative Gaetz sent the Committee a copy of a social media post from Mr. Dorworth regarding his lawsuit against Victim A, in which he had accused her of being part of a conspiracy to defame him. In that post, Mr. Dorworth discussed his recent settlement with Victim A (in which no funds were exchanged). He asserted that he had "succeeded" in proving that Victim A "lied" about him, and that "[s]he didn't just lie about me, she lied about Gaetz as well in a federal criminal investigation that resulted in no charges against the congressman because our false-accuser has no credibility and had no evidence for the crime that didn't occur." The same day, Mr. Dorworth revised his post (after Victim A's attorneys contacted his attorneys) to remove his claim that he succeeded in proving the Victim A had lied but maintaining his assertion that she falsely accused Representative Gaetz. Mr. Dorworth testified to the Committee that he himself was not present for the July 15, 2017, party at his own home, despite Victim A's assertions to the contrary. After the Committee's interview, and after he settled his lawsuit against Victim A, Mr. Dorworth was deposed and confronted with cell phone records showing that he was in fact at his residence during the party. Mr. Dorworth stated, "I don't have an answer to these questions" and "I am not going to opine on cell phone data when I don't know anything about [it]. . . . I don't know. I do not believe I was there. . . . There could be a million reasons for that." As the questions about his cell phone pinging from a tower less than a mile from his home continued, Mr. Dorworth became irritated, informing the attorney "I'm telling you that I was not at that party. So if you believe those [phone records] somehow impute that I was or that they make it just undeniable, then that is certainly your belief." The Committee requested, through counsel, that Mr. Dorworth clarify his testimony regarding his whereabouts on the evening of July 15, 2017; his counsel did not respond.

4. Representative Gaetz's Response to the Allegations of Sexual Misconduct and Illicit Drug Use

Representative Gaetz categorically stated to the Committee that the allegations he "may have engaged in sexual misconduct including violations of federal laws relating to sex trafficking

---

[102] 18(a) Interview of Victim A. *See also* 18(a) Interview of Woman 4 ("[T]he state everyone was in . . . made me assume that [Representative Gaetz] was probably on [some drugs].").

[103] 18(a) Interview of Victim A (A: [W]hen[] I first got to that party [] I wasn't that drunk at the beginning of the party, and [] those two memories are [] so huge in my head... Q: [I]s there any chance that you are misremembering whether or not you engaged in sexual activity with Matt Gaetz when you were 17 years old? A: No.). Mr. Greenberg claimed to have witnessed Victim A having sex with Representative Gaetz at the home of Individual 1 when she was 17 years old; however, Victim A did not recall such an instance occurring. Victim A also had hazy memories of other occasions on which she saw Representative Gaetz.

and state laws relating to prostitution and statutory rape," were "false" and that "[t]hese allegations were investigated by the Department of Justice and the investigation was completely dropped." He also repeatedly, incorrectly stated that the DOJ investigation "exonerated" him. Representative Gaetz did not provide any explanation for his assertion that the allegations of state law violations were false, even though those violations were not within the jurisdiction of DOJ. He also denied the allegations that he used illicit drugs.[104]

The Committee provided Representative Gaetz with the names of 15 women who were alleged to have received payments from him or on his behalf relating to sexual misconduct and illicit drug use, as well as the approximate payment amounts and transaction years, but he did not provide any explanation for those payments. Representative Gaetz responded publicly to allegations that his payments to women were for sex by stating that "someone is trying to recategorize my generosity to ex-girlfriends as something more untoward."[105] He also repeatedly denied having ever paid for sex.[106] When given the opportunity to put that assertion in writing in this matter, however, Representative Gaetz refused to respond, asserting that "asking about [his] sexual history as a single man with adult women is a bridge too far."

Representative Gaetz did broadly address the allegation that he engaged in sexual activity with a minor; he asserted in his September 26, 2024, letter to the Committee: "Your correspondence of September 4 asks whether I have engaged in sexual activity with any individual under 18. The answer to this question is unequivocally NO. You can apply this response to every version of this question, in every forum."[107] The Committee's September 4 letter, however, specifically asked him whether he was present at the July 15, 2017, party at Mr. Dorworth's, whether he ever engaged in sexual activity with Victim A and when, and whether he ever gave Victim A money (directly or indirectly) and if so, for what purpose. Representative Gaetz did not answer any of those questions.

---

[104] *See, e.g.*, @FmrRepMattGaetz, X (formerly Twitter) (Sept. 26, 2024, 12:29 p.m.), https://twitter.com/FmrRepMattGaetz/status/1839341409582846196 (hereinafter, September 26 X Post) ("I have not used drugs which are illegal, absent some law allowing use in a jurisdiction of the United States. I have not used 'illicit' drugs, which I consider to be drugs unlawful for medical or over-the-counter use everywhere in the United States.").

[105] *See, e.g.*, Will Steakin, *Witness Tells House Ethics Committee That Matt Gaetz Paid Her for Sex: Sources*, ABC News (June 19, 2024), https://abcnews.go.com/US/witness-tells-house-ethics-committee-matt-gaetz-paid/story?id=111217102; *Mar. 30 NYT Article*.

[106] *Id.*

[106] *February 14 ABC Article* (a spokesperson for the congressman stated, "Rep. Gaetz has never paid for sex."); Michael S. Schmidt and Katie Benner, *Indicted Gaetz Associate is Said to be Cooperating with Justice Dept.*, The New York Times (Apr. 13, 2021), https://www.nytimes.com/2021/04/13/us/politics/joel-greenberg-matt-gaetz.html (a spokesperson for Representative Gaetz stated, "Congressman Gaetz has never paid for sex"); Marc Caputo, *The Congressman and His Wingman*, Politico (Apr. 6, 2021), https://politico.com/states/florida/story/2021/04/06/the-congressman-and-his-wingman-1371840 (hereinafter *April 6 Politico Article*) ("I have never paid for sex"); Representative Matt Gaetz, *Rep. Matt Gaetz: The Swamp is Out to Drown Me with False Charges, but I'm Not Giving Up*, The Washington Examiner (Apr. 5, 2021), https://www.washingtonexaminer.com/opinion/1933067/rep-matt-gaetz-the-swamp-is-out-to-drown-me-with-false-charges-but-im-not-giving-up/ (hereinafter *April 5 Washington Examiner Article*) ("[L]et me address the allegations against me directly. First, I have never, ever paid for sex.").

[107] *See* Appendix A.

B. Allegations Relating to the House Gift Rule

In 2021, news outlets reported that federal investigators were reviewing the 2018 Bahamas trip.[108] According to these reports, the trip was paid for by an associate of Representative Gaetz with connections to the medical marijuana industry, who allegedly also paid for female escorts to accompany them on the trip.[109] The only other male attendee was also connected to the medical marijuana industry. According to press reports, DOJ was investigating allegations that the trip may have been part of an illegal influence effort on behalf of the medical marijuana industry.[110]

As discussed above, the Bahamas trip took place from September 13 to 16, 2018, and included Representative Gaetz, two other men, and six women. Representative Gaetz flew on a commercial airline from Washington, D.C. to the Bahamas on September 13, 2018. Representative Gaetz's associate paid for a vacation rental for the group but told the Committee that Representative Gaetz paid for various expenses in the Bahamas, such as meals, and that these expenses covered Representative Gaetz's share of the vacation rental. No other individuals recalled whether Representative Gaetz paid for their meals, vacation rental, or other activities on this trip, with the exception of his then-girlfriend. No one recalled Representative Gaetz making cash payments, and his bank statements and credit card records do not show any transactions on these dates occurring in the Bahamas, nor large withdrawals of cash during or in advance of the trip. On September 16, 2018, Representative Gaetz flew on his associate's private plane from the Bahamas to Orlando, along with three female passengers between 20 to 29 years old.[111]

C. Allegations Related to Misuse of Official Resources

As discussed above, in early 2018, Representative Gaetz met a woman through Mr. Greenberg; the same night they met, they had sex and Mr. Greenberg sent her money. At that first meeting, the woman also told Representative Gaetz she needed a new passport for an upcoming trip. She did not initially know Representative Gaetz was a congressman, but he connected her with his then-Chief of Staff, who worked with the State Department's congressional liaison to secure a passport appointment for the woman within days of their first meeting. An individual from the Department of State, Miami Passport Agency sent the Chief of Staff an e-mail confirming "an appointment for your constituent," which the Chief of Staff then forwarded to the woman, who lived in Orlando, Florida—outside of Representative Gaetz's congressional district.[112]

The woman acknowledged to the Committee that the money she received from Mr. Greenberg was sent on behalf of Representative Gaetz but denied that the money was compensation for their sexual encounter. Instead, she said the $1,000 she received from Mr.

---

[108] Major Garrett et al., *Matt Gaetz Trip to Bahamas is Part of Federal Probe into Sex Trafficking, Sources Say*, CBS NEWS (Apr. 8, 2021), https://www.cbsnews.com/news/matt-gaetz-bahamas-trip-federal-probe-sex-trafficking.
[109] *Id.*
[110] Evan Perez et al., *Gaetz Probe Includes Scrutiny of Potential Public Corruption Tied to Medical Marijuana Industry*, CNN (Apr. 23, 2021), https://www.cnn.com/2021/04/23/politics/gaetz-probe-public-corruption-medical-marijuana/index.html. The Committee did not find any evidence that the trip was intended as a quid pro quo or gratuity for Representative Gaetz's official actions.
[111] Exhibit 10.
[112] 18(a) Interview of Woman 3.

Greenberg was to assist her with transportation costs to go to the Miami passport office from Orlando.[113] The woman spent $195 to obtain her new passport prior to her trip—a standard $60 fee for an in-person appointment, plus $135 for the passport. She continued to meet up with Representative Gaetz on other occasions, during which they engaged in sexual activity.

The Committee reviewed other records relating to passport assistance requests from the office of Representative Gaetz. It was unusual for the Chief of Staff to process requests for expedited passports from constituents; those casework matters were typically handled by district staff. The Committee also received evidence that Representative Gaetz tasked the Chief of Staff with assisting Mr. Greenberg on occasion. The Chief of Staff was no longer employed in Representative Gaetz's office at the time of the Committee's review and did not respond to communications from the Committee.

D. Obstruction of the Committee's Investigation

On May 23, 2023, the Committee informed Representative Gaetz that it had reauthorized an investigation into several allegations, including sexual misconduct and illicit drug use, and sent Representative Gaetz a narrowly tailored request for information seeking specific documents related to allegations squarely within the Committee's jurisdiction—namely, violations related to the House Gift Rule or bribery and improper images on the House floor. The request for information also asked for "any other information that you believe may be relevant" to the matter as a whole. In response, Representative Gaetz began sending letters to the Chairman and Ranking Member asserting, among other things, that the Committee's requests for a two-week response time and signed declaration under oath (both of which are standard practice for the Committee) were unreasonable and that he was being treated differently than other Members of Congress. Representative Gaetz indicated that the Committee's request was overly burdensome, as he would need to sort through six years' worth of records, across various accounts. In these letters, he also began making demands of the Committee in exchange for his "good faith" cooperation while suggesting that the Committee was being "weaponized" against him for various changing reasons.

The Chairman and Ranking Member granted Representative Gaetz an extension through August 11, 2023, to respond to the request for information, and explained the Committee's standard practices.[114] Representative Gaetz missed the deadline, and stated he would only produce

---

[113] *See* Section IV.C *supra*.

[114] The July 19, 2023, letter explained, among other things, that the Committee determined that public allegations raised against Representative Gaetz should be reviewed, consistent with longstanding practice regarding public allegations of sexual misconduct (*see, e.g.*, Comm. on Ethics, Statement of the Chairwoman and Ranking Member of the Committee on Ethics Regarding Representative John Conyers, Jr. (Nov. 21, 2017), https://ethics.house.gov/press-release/statement-chairwoman-and-ranking-member-committee-ethics-regarding-representative-jo-1; Comm. on Ethics, Statement of the Chairwoman and Ranking Member of the Committee on Ethics Regarding Representative Ruben Kihuen (Dec. 15, 2017), https://ethics.house.gov/press-release/statement-chairwoman-and-ranking-member-committee-ethics-regarding-representative-8; Comm. on Ethics, Statement of the Chairwoman and Ranking Member of the Committee on Ethics Regarding Representative Patrick Meehan (Jan. 22, 2018), https://ethics.house.gov/press-release/statement-chairwoman-and-ranking-member-committee-ethics-regarding-representative-12; Comm. on Ethics, Statement of Chairman and Ranking Member of the Committee on Ethics Regarding Delegate Michael F.Q. San Nicolas (Oct. 24, 2019), https://ethics.house.gov/press-

documents in-person at his district office.[115] The Chairman and Ranking Member responded again, giving him an extension through September 28, 2023, to comply with the request for information and reiterating the Committee's standard practices. Representative Gaetz again missed the deadline, ultimately producing three pages that were not fully responsive to the request for information on October 2, 2023. In his response, Representative Gaetz produced his "boarding passes and itinerary" used for the 2018 Bahamas trip, which he also stated he "paid for personally." However, the boarding passes and itinerary only show his flight to the Bahamas and not his return (as discussed above, Representative Gaetz flew out of the Bahamas via private plane). Representative Gaetz intentionally omitted information relating to his return transportation, indicating in later correspondence that, because the Committee's request was for documents "related to actual or planned travel *to* the Bahamas," (emphasis added), he should not be expected to have produced records of his transportation *from* that location. When the Committee noted that any documents involving his transportation from the Bahamas were clearly "related to" the travel at issue, his response made clear that he was not willing to provide good faith responses:

> [D]oes the Committee also have interest in every dollar I spent in the Bahamas on food, refreshments and other travel provisions such as sunscreen? I ask because your request is unclear, unrelated to House Rules, and more than a bit nosey. I can represent to the Committee that no funds of mine were expended in the Bahamas for "illicit drug use" or sexual misconduct.

Despite frequently suggesting he had insufficient opportunities to respond to the allegations against him, Representative Gaetz sent more than a dozen letters to the Chairman and Ranking Member throughout the Committee's review. In addition to alleging that the Committee's process was being "weaponized" against him, Representative Gaetz repeatedly alleged that the Committee Members and staff were leaking information to the press, that the Committee's non-partisan staff were actually acting as Democrats, or that the Committee was working on behalf of former-Speaker Kevin McCarthy. He also demanded to know the sources of the allegations against him and argued that the Committee's investigation should be closed because DOJ had "exonerated" him.

On May 20, 2024, the Committee requested Representative Gaetz provide availability for an interview to be conducted sometime in the first two weeks of June; the interview would be an

---

releases/statement-chairman-and-ranking-member-committee-ethics-regarding-delegate-michael-f-q; Comm. on Ethics, Statement of Chairman and Ranking Member of the Committee on Ethics Regarding Representative Katie Hill (Oct. 23, 2019), https://ethics.house.gov/press-releases/statement-chairman-and-ranking-member-committee-ethics-regarding-representative-katie; Comm. on Ethics, Statement of Chairman and Ranking Member of the Committee on Ethics Regarding Representative Alcee Hastings (Nov. 14, 2019), https://ethics.house.gov/press-releases/statement-chairman-and-ranking-member-committee-ethics-regarding-representative-alcee; Comm. on Ethics, Statement of the Chairman and Ranking Member of the Committee on Ethics Regarding Representative Tom Reed (Apr. 9, 2021), https://ethics.house.gov/press-releases/statement-chairman-and-ranking-member-committee-ethics-regarding-representative-tom).

[115] As Representative Gaetz is undoubtedly aware, it is common practice to provide materials responsive to a congressional request via e-mail, courier, or a secure cloud-based platform. In fact, he provided documents via e-mail in the Committee's prior investigation into his conduct. Comm. on Ethics, *In the Matter of Allegations Relating to Representative Matt Gaetz*, H. Rept. 116-479, 116th Cong., 2d Sess. (2020) (hereinafter *Gaetz*).

opportunity for Representative Gaetz to answer questions about and respond to the allegations.[116] In that letter, the Committee appended a fulsome list of allegations involving Representative Gaetz, to ensure his awareness of all allegations before the Committee. On May 24, 2024, Representative Gaetz responded to the Committee's letter. He demanded the Committee investigate "leaks" to the press prior to him submitting for an interview and argued (incorrectly) that the Committee could not subpoena his testimony unless it impaneled an investigative subcommittee.[117] He also referred to "voluminous documentary evidence" he produced to the Committee that he claimed showed his innocence and categorically denied all the allegations.

On June 17, 2024, the Committee informed Representative Gaetz that it would be both expanding and narrowing the scope of its investigation into allegations involving him. The letter also requested evidence that DOJ had "exonerated" him,[118] any records previously produced to DOJ, and any other documents he believed the Committee should have already received comprising the "voluminous" evidence he claimed to have provided. Finally, the letter reiterated the Committee's request that Representative Gaetz appear for a voluntary interview and reminded him that, pursuant to Committee Rule 10(a), it would consider whether to use compulsory process to obtain his testimony.

Representative Gaetz responded on June 24, 2024, stating that he would need additional time to review "over ten thousand records" he had previously submitted to DOJ.[119] He also reiterated his requests that the Committee provide him with confidential information about its investigative sources, as well as regarding any investigation of disclosures in the press. He then publicly called the Committee's investigation "frivolous" and said it was an "obvious fact that

---

[116] The letter also noted that, should Representative Gaetz not submit to a voluntary interview, the Committee may use its compulsory process to obtain his testimony. *See* Committee Rule 10(a)(1).

[117] The Committee's subpoena authority is not related to whether it establishes an investigative subcommittee, which is only one procedural path for investigation by the Committee. *See* House Rule XI, cl. 2(m); Committee Rule 10(a)(1); *see also, e.g.*, Comm. on Ethics, *In the Matter of Allegations Relating to Delegate Michael F. Q. San Nicolas*, H. Rept. 117-387, 117th Cong., 2d Sess. (2022) (hereinafter *San Nicolas*) (ISC issued a subpoena after the Delegate declined a voluntary interview and did not meaningfully respond to several opportunities to provide a written statement to address the allegations against him); Comm. on Ethics, *In the Matter of Allegations Relating to Laura Richardson*, H. Rept. 112-642, 112th Cong., 2d Sess. (2012) (hereinafter *Richardson*); Comm. on Standards of Official Conduct, *In the Matter of Representative Charles B. Rangel*, H. Rept. 111-161, 111th Cong., 2d Sess. (2010) (Member agreed to voluntarily produce documents after staff informed him the Committee issued a subpoena and the subpoena was not served); *McDermott;* Comm. on Standards of Official Conduct, *Investigation of Allegations Related to Improper Conduct Involving Members and Current or Former House Pages*, H. Rept. 109-733, 109th Cong., 2d Sess. (2006) (subpoenas served to preserve documents at the outset of the investigation, rather than compel production of documents); Comm. on Standards of Official Conduct, *Investigation of Certain Allegations Related to Voting on the Medicare Prescription Drug, Improvement, and Modernization Act of 2003*, H. Rept. 108-722, 108th Cong., 2d Sess. (2004) (subpoenaing Representative Nick Smith, the only Member in the investigation who declined to voluntarily interview); Comm. on Standards of Official Conduct, *In the Matter of Representative E.G. "Bud" Shuster*, H. Rept. 106-979, 106th Cong., 2d Sess. at 94-98 (2000); Comm. on Standards of Official Conduct, *In the Matter of Representative Barbara-Rose Collins*, H. Rept. 104-876, 104th Cong., 2d Sess. (1997). Furthermore, an investigative subcommittee is not the most common process through which the Committee conducts its investigations; most Committee investigations are conducted pursuant to Committee Rule 18(a), as in this matter.

[118] *See* Section II *supra* (regarding DOJ's non-cooperation with the Committee).

[119] Representative Gaetz did not explain in his letter why he has not produced those 10,000 records to the Committee despite having been informed of the Committee's reauthorized investigation more than a year prior.

every investigation into me ends the same way: my exoneration."[120] Representative Gaetz ultimately produced some additional documents to the Committee through early September, although it is not clear how many of those documents had been previously produced to DOJ. The Committee also invited Representative Gaetz to clarify the relevancy of the records he produced, most of which did not appear to be responsive to the Committee's request, to which he stated only that he was prioritizing the evidence that most clearly proved his innocence. Representative Gaetz also falsely stated in a letter to the Committee, which he shared in a public social media post, that he had "voluntarily produced tens of thousands of records." To the contrary, Representative Gaetz provided only a couple hundred records, more than 90 percent of which was either irrelevant or publicly available. Despite multiple extensions from the Committee to review and produce responsive records from the "ten thousand" he claimed he would review, Representative Gaetz ultimately declared he would "no longer cooperate" with the Committee in the public letter.[121]

The Committee also reviewed allegations that Representative Gaetz may have sought to tamper with witness testimony in connection with its investigation or the DOJ's investigation. DOJ refused to provide a copy of an audio recording in which Representative Gaetz discussed the DOJ's inquiry with one of the women he paid for sex.

While the Committee did not find documentary evidence that Representative Gaetz directly acted to prevent any woman from testifying before DOJ or the Committee, some women cited a fear of retaliation from the congressman when declining to speak on the record with the Committee.

---

[120] @FmrRepMattGaetz, X (formerly Twitter) (June 17, 2024, 4:41 PM), https://twitter.com/FmrRepMattGaetz/status/1802803825826304266. DOJ did not characterize the closure of their investigation into Representative Gaetz as an "exoneration" to the Committee. Representative Gaetz has also repeatedly claimed that "there are exactly zero credible (or even non-credible) accusers willing to come forward by name and state on the public record that I behaved improperly toward them." *April 5 Washington Examiner Article*; *see also* Jake Tapper, Rep. Matt Gaetz on Efforts to Oust House Speaker, CNN, at 6:10 (May 6, 2024), https://cnn.com/videos/politics/2024/05/06/the-lead-matt-gaetz-speaker-johnson-oust-niger-troops-jake-tapper.cnn (calling the allegations an "urban legend"); *April 6 Politico Article*. However, DOJ's investigation involved grand jury hearings, during which many of the women that the Committee contacted or interviewed testified, in addition to conducting depositions under penalty of perjury with the Committee.
[121] @FmrRepMattGaetz, September 26 X Post. Representative Gaetz also provided a copy of the letter and its attachments to the Committee after having made his post public.

V. FINDINGS

A. The Committee Found Representative Gaetz Violated State Laws Related to Sexual Misconduct

1. The Committee Did Not Find that Representative Gaetz Violated Federal Sex Trafficking Laws

The Committee did not obtain substantial evidence that Representative Gaetz violated federal sex trafficking laws. Transportation of an individual for purposes of commercial sex could violate such laws if the individual was a minor, or if the sexual activity occurred through force, fraud, or coercion.

Representative Gaetz was alleged in news reports to have paid a minor to engage in sexual activity and travel with him on a trip to the Bahamas in September 2018. However, the youngest person who traveled with him and his associates was 18 years old at the time of the trip. Further, she and the other women who attended the Bahamas trip did not recall being paid for sexual activity on that occasion. One woman testified that she was not paid for sex on the trip, although she did have sex with Representative Gaetz, because "the trip itself was more so the payment."[122]

As discussed above, there is evidence that Representative Gaetz paid women to travel to New York and Washington, D.C. for commercial sex. At the time, each of the women was over the age of 18. While Representative Gaetz's relationship with these women involved an exploitative power imbalance, the Committee does not have reason to believe that he used force, fraud, or coercion as those terms apply under the applicable laws.

2. The Committee Found that Representative Gaetz Engaged in Commercial Sex

There is substantial evidence that Representative Gaetz paid women for sex, and had others pay women for sex on his behalf. The Committee heard testimony from over half a dozen witnesses who attended parties, events, and trips with Representative Gaetz from 2017-2020. Nearly every young woman that the Committee interviewed confirmed that she was paid for sex by, or on behalf of, Representative Gaetz. A few of the women characterized their relationship differently, describing a date-for-hire arrangement that may not necessarily implicate state prostitution laws. Even assuming the payments to those particular women would not violate prostitution laws, the Committee found evidence that Representative Gaetz spent tens of thousands of dollars on other women with whom he had a shared understanding that they would be compensated for sexual activity with him. There were potentially additional amounts spent on commercial sex that could not be specifically identified either because payments were made in cash or through intermediaries. The Committee's record thus indicates that Representative Gaetz enticed and procured women to engage in sexual activity for hire and purchased the services of women engaging in sexual activity for hire, in violation of Florida state law.

---

[122] 18(a) Interview of Woman 5.

Representative Gaetz refused to answer the Committee's questions about his payments to women, despite opportunities to do so in sworn testimony or in writing. While he has been unwilling to address the allegations under oath, Representative Gaetz has made several public statements regarding the allegations under the Committee's review, including that his "generosity to ex-girlfriends" is being misconstrued and that he has "never, ever paid for sex." The Committee found this to be untrue.

Members are required to uphold the laws of the United States and all governments therein, and never be a party to their evasion.[123] Through his violations of state prostitution laws, Representative Gaetz acted contrary to this ethical obligation.[124] Representative Gaetz took advantage of the economic vulnerability of young women to lure them into sexual activity for which they received an average of a few hundred dollars after each encounter. Such behavior is not "generosity to ex-girlfriends," and it does not reflect creditably upon the House. The Committee thus found Representative Gaetz to be in violation of House Rule XXIII, clause 1.

3. The Committee Found that Representative Gaetz Violated Florida's Statutory Rape Law

There is substantial evidence that Representative Gaetz engaged in sexual activity with a 17-year-old girl. The Committee received credible testimony from Victim A herself, as well as multiple individuals corroborating the allegation. Several of those witnesses have also testified under oath before a federal grand jury and in a civil litigation. Representative Gaetz denied the allegation but refused to testify under oath. He has publicly stated that Victim A "doesn't exist" and that he has not "had sex with a 17-year-old since I was 17."[125] The Committee found that to be untrue and determined that there is substantial evidence that Representative Gaetz had sex with Victim A in July 2017, when she was 17 years old, and he was 35. Representative Gaetz's actions were in violation of Florida's statutory rape law.

Representative Gaetz has suggested that the allegations against him have been manufactured and that Mr. Greenberg and Victim A are not credible. The Committee has acknowledged that Mr. Greenberg's credibility is in doubt. The Committee received additional evidence from Mr. Greenberg that is not included in this Report, much of it salacious but unverifiable, although consistent with the nature of the conduct that the Committee learned of from other witnesses. The Committee found no reason to doubt the credibility of Victim A. Representative Gaetz has suggested the fact that she has, through her attorneys, expressed an intention to seek civil redress against him for raping her means that she has a financial motive that undermines the veracity of her claims. The Committee reviewed a letter from counsel to Victim A to counsel for Representative Gaetz, which stated she intended to "pursue claims against

---

[123] Code of Ethics for Government Service, ¶ 2.
[124] While the statute of limitations to bring state law charges against Representative Gaetz has long passed, that limitations period is not applicable to the Committee's findings. Pursuant to Committee Rule 18(d) and House Rule XI, cl. 3(b)(3), the Committee's investigative authority extends to any violations occurring since the third previous Congress (in this matter, since January 2017).
[125] *Carlson Interview*; *April 6 Politico Article*.

[Representative Gaetz] including child sex trafficking and statutory rape."[126] Regardless of whether Victim A had any pecuniary motive in sending such a communication, she cooperated with DOJ's investigation for years and was let down by the justice system when reports circulated that DOJ would be unlikely to pursue charges against Representative Gaetz.[127] Victim A is entitled to all of the protections and remedies available to her under civil laws, and her intention to pursue claims against Representative Gaetz and others does not negate her credibility. Moreover, as discussed above, the Committee obtained testimony and documentary evidence from other witnesses corroborating the allegations.

Representative Gaetz's statutory rape of Victim A was a violation of Florida law, the Code of Official Conduct, and the Code of Ethics for Government Service. The Committee received evidence that Representative Gaetz did not learn that Victim A was 17 years old until more than a month after their first sexual encounters. However, statutory rape is a strict liability crime. After he learned that Victim A was a minor, he maintained contact and less than 6 months after she turned 18, he met up with her again for commercial sex. When Mr. Greenberg was prosecuted for sex trafficking the same individual, Representative Gaetz denied that she existed.[128] His conduct reflects discreditably upon the House.

B. The Committee Found Representative Gaetz Used Illegal Drugs

There is substantial evidence that Representative Gaetz used cocaine, ecstasy, and marijuana. At least two women saw Representative Gaetz using cocaine and ecstasy at different events.[129] Even more women understood him to regularly be using ecstasy. There is also ample evidence that Representative Gaetz purchased and used marijuana; he appears to have set up a pseudonymous e-mail account from his House office in the Capitol complex for the purpose of purchasing marijuana. Representative Gaetz denied using illicit drugs in written correspondence to the Committee.

---

[126] Letter from counsel to Victim A to counsel to Representative Gaetz (Dec. 30, 2022). Representative Gaetz provided this letter to the Committee but did not produce subsequent correspondence showing that his counsel engaged in discussions regarding a potential pre-filing settlement. Over three months, Representative Gaetz's counsel delayed Victim A's counsel from filing her lawsuit by engaging in what were ultimately unsuccessful settlement discussions, in part due to "constrain[ts] by [Representative Gaetz's] limited [financial] resources."

[127] *See, e.g.*, Evan Perez and Hannah Rabinowitz, *DOJ Prosecutors Recommend Against Charging Rep. Gaetz in Sex-Trafficking Probe*, CNN (Sept. 23, 2022), https://www.cnn.com/2022/09/23/politics/matt-gaetz-justice-department-probe/index.html. Victim A also noted in her response in the civil litigation that she would not be precluded from filing counterclaims against Mr. Dorworth: "the Complaint improperly seeks to preempt any claims [Victim A] may have against Mr. Dorworth for raping and trafficking her by making a threadbare request for expansive declaratory judgment." Mot. to Dismiss Complaint by Victim A, *Christopher Dorworth v. Joel Greenberg, et al.*, No. 6:23-cv-00871 (M.D. Fla.). Victim A settled with Mr. Dorworth in August 2024. On the same date as the settlement, Representative Gaetz produced a publicly available Facebook post by Mr. Dorworth as evidence that Victim A was "not credible." Letter from Representative Matt Gaetz to Chairman Michael Guest and Ranking Member Susan Wild, Committee on Ethics (Aug. 2, 2024). Shortly thereafter, Mr. Dorworth edited the post to remove various assertions, including allegations that Victim A was a "prostitute." Representative Gaetz argued that the initial Facebook post was "dispositive" in showing Victim A's "unreliability."

[128] Caroline Linton, *Matt Gaetz denies relationship with a 17-year-old and says he's a victim of attempted extortion*, CBS NEWS (Mar. 31, 2021), https://www.cbsnews.com/news/matt-gaetz-denies-inappropriate-sexual-relationship-17-year-old-investigation/ ("The person doesn't exist. I have not had a relationship with a 17-year-old.").

[129] Mr. Greenberg also stated he witnessed Representative Gaetz take ecstasy and cocaine.

Members of Congress are not required to undergo the same background check process as other government officials who obtain a security clearance. That process includes answering questions about use of illegal drugs in the seven preceding years. Representative Gaetz used illegal drugs on numerous occasions between 2017 and 2020, in violation of state laws. The Committee also received evidence that Representative Gaetz and his associates provided drugs to women to facilitate the sexual misconduct described above. Representative Gaetz's conduct violated paragraph 2 of the Code of Ethics for Government Service and clause 1 of the Code of Official Conduct.

C. The Committee Found that Representative Gaetz Violated the House Gift Rule

There is substantial evidence that Representative Gaetz received impermissible gifts in connection with his travel to the Bahamas in September 2018. Specifically, Representative Gaetz accepted travel via a private plane and other travel costs. Contrary to Representative Gaetz's claims that he provided "substantial" evidence to the Committee "demonstrating his innocence" on this allegation, he provided no evidence showing how he paid for any travel costs other than his flight to the Bahamas, despite being given multiple opportunities to do so.

As discussed above, Representative Gaetz's associate provided the lodging and return flight via private plane. Representative Gaetz accepted this gift without first seeking approval from the Committee.[130] The Gift Rule requires Members to apply to the Committee for a waiver to accept gifts of personal friendship with a fair market value over a threshold amount.[131] For travel via private plane, the Committee has provided extensive guidance; less than a year after Representative Gaetz's flight from the Bahamas trip, the Committee circulated a reminder about that guidance to the House community, noting that "[p]ractically any flight on a non-commercial aircraft will exceed $250 in value and hence will require Committee approval."[132] The flight, lodging, meal and "entertainment" expenses on the Bahamas trip that were incurred but not paid by Representative Gaetz were well in excess of the personal friendship threshold.[133] The Committee also found evidence that Representative Gaetz impermissibly accepted private plane travel on other occasions. Representative Gaetz failed to disclose the Bahamas travel gift, as well as other private flights he has taken on his associates' private planes, on his Financial Disclosure forms.

Accordingly, the Committee found that Representative Gaetz violated House Rule XXV, clause 5, by accepting impermissible gifts. Consistent with the Committee's longstanding

---

[130] The personal hospitality exception to the Gift Rule would not be applicable in this matter because Representative Gaetz did not stay at a personal residence of the gift-giver.
[131] *See Young* (finding that on at least three occasions, although Representative Young "may have been permitted to accept the gift of travel under the personal friendship exception to the gift rule at the time," because he did not seek approval from the Committee, "the exception was inapplicable" and he was not permitted to accept the travel).
[132] Comm. on Ethics, *Non-Commercial Aircraft Travel* (Apr. 10, 2019), https://ethics.house.gov/sites/ethics.house.gov/files/Private%20Plane%20pinksheet%20FINAL.pdf.
[133] Had Representative Gaetz applied for a waiver, the Committee would have considered multiple factors including the nature of the friendship, which could have involved questions related to their joint interest in and past efforts towards lobbying for medical marijuana.

precedent, Representative Gaetz would be required to repay the value of the gifts and amend his Financial Disclosure statements to disclose receipt of the gifts.[134]

D. The Committee Found Representative Gaetz Dispensed Special Privileges and Favors to Individuals with Whom He Had a Personal Relationship

The Committee found substantial evidence that Representative Gaetz used the power of his office to assist a woman with whom he was engaged in a sexual relationship in obtaining an expedited passport. The woman was not his constituent, and the case was not handled in the same manner as similar passport assistance cases. Accordingly, the Committee found Representative Gaetz violated House regulations and laws requiring the use of official resources for representational purposes, and paragraph 5 of the Code of Ethics for Government Service, which prohibits the dispensing of special favors and privileges.

E. The Committee Found Representative Gaetz Sought to Obstruct Its Investigation of His Conduct

The Committee found substantial evidence that Representative Gaetz engaged in obstructive conduct with respect to the Committee's investigation. Representative Gaetz pointed to evidence that would "exonerate" him yet failed to produce any such materials.[135] Representative Gaetz continuously sought to deflect, deter, or mislead the Committee in order to prevent his actions from being exposed. This was most notable with respect to the Committee's specific requests regarding the Bahamas trip; as discussed above, Representative Gaetz intentionally withheld information relating to his return trip via private plane. Representative Gaetz clearly understood that he had acted contrary to House Rules by accepting private plane travel but chose to try to cover up his actions rather than comply with the Committee's request.

Despite asserting he wanted an opportunity to address the allegations against him, Representative Gaetz declined to provide testimony voluntarily and did not appear when subpoenaed.[136] Representative Gaetz was also provided ample time to review and produce documents requested at various points in the Committee's investigation, yet he produced only a

---

[134] Comm. on Ethics, *In the Matter of Allegations Relating to Representative Madison Cawthorn*, H. Rept. 117-591, 117th Cong., 2d Sess. (2022); Comm. on Ethics, *In the Matter of Allegations Relating to Representative Bobby L. Rush*, H. Rept. 115-618, 115th Cong., 2d Sess. (2018); *Young*.

[135] Representative Gaetz pointed to news articles, the lack of a DOJ indictment, evidence that Mr. Greenberg is an unreliable witness, and a letter from a jailhouse informant as exonerating. However, he did not produce any contemporaneous documents that showed he did not engage in the conduct under investigation, such as his own text messages, peer-to-peer payment platform records, calendar entries from relevant time frames, *etc*. In an X (formerly Twitter) post, Representative Gaetz suggested, without actual knowledge, that the Committee's "star witness" is Mr. Greenberg. As noted at several points in this Report, the Committee agreed with Representative Gaetz that Mr. Greenberg is not entirely credible and sought evidence from numerous other sources. Representative Gaetz also produced a letter from a jailhouse informant and a subsequent interview conducted by "two former federal investigators." However, those investigators were not objective third-party interviewees; rather, they appear to have been hired by Representative Gaetz's counsel. @FmrRepMatt Gaetz September 26 X Post.

[136] The Rules of the House do not apply any standard to service of process, unlike the Federal Rules of Civil Procedure, and other individuals, including Members of Congress, have been served subpoenas by e-mail in recent Congresses. As noted, Representative Gaetz acknowledged that he received the subpoena from the Committee.

handful of non-public documents to the Committee.[137] These documents were largely irrelevant, corresponding to time periods after most of the relevant conduct occurred. Likewise, Representative Gaetz informed the Committee that he would "welcome" the opportunity to respond to written questions, and the Committee then sent a list of 16 questions. After requesting an extension to respond to written questions, which was granted, it appears that Representative Gaetz used that time to craft a public letter mischaracterizing the Committee's requests and asserting he would "no longer" voluntarily cooperate, despite his uncooperative approach throughout the review.[138] His actions undermine not only his claims that he had exculpatory information to provide, but also his claims that he intended to cooperate with the Committee in good faith. It is apparent that Representative Gaetz's assertions were nothing more than attempts to delay the Committee's investigation.

Representative Gaetz routinely ignored or significantly delayed producing relevant information requested by the Committee. His failure to respond required the Committee to issue subpoenas to financial institutions for Representative Gaetz's financial records related to alleged transactions. Those records show that Representative Gaetz bought and sold stocks and cryptocurrencies from a trading account he opened in March 2021.[139] Some of the trades were below the $1,000 reporting threshold but others were not. Representative Gaetz not only failed to file the required Periodic Transaction Reports, but he also failed to disclose the transactions in his annual Financial Disclosure Statement. The Committee's longstanding practice is not to take enforcement action where a failure to file required disclosures is inadvertent, but because of his lack of cooperation the Committee was unable to determine the reason the transactions were not disclosed.

The Committee reminded Representative Gaetz of his duty of diligence and candor to the Committee.[140] Representative Gaetz's response was to suggest that the Committee had a duty of candor to *him* and must reveal the confidential sources supporting the allegations against him. The Committee's rules prevent such disclosures. Moreover, the Committee had serious concerns that Representative Gaetz might retaliate against individuals who cooperated with the Committee. In 2020, the Committee admonished Representative Gaetz for his conduct towards a witness in a congressional proceeding, finding that he acted in violation of the Code of Official Conduct for a public statement that was perceived by some as a threat towards a witness.[141] In that matter, the Committee did not find sufficient evidence to conclude that Representative Gaetz had the requisite

---

[137] Representative Gaetz further asserted that he would need to ascertain whether "privilege or confidentiality" applies to documents that he previously produced to DOJ. The Committee is not aware of any privileges that would permit withholding documents that were previously produced to another governmental entity, and there is no basis to withhold documents for "confidentiality."
[138] @FmrRepMattGaetz September 26 X Post.
[139] Personal Checking Account #1 (showing over 50 purchases of stock or cryptocurrency on Coinbase and Robinhood from March 2021 through June 2021 in amounts ranging from $100 to $3,105.62).
[140] Comm. on Ethics, *In the Matter of Allegations Relating to Representative George Santos*, H. Rept. 118-274, 118th Cong., 1st Sess. 55 (2023); *San Nicolas* at 5; Comm. on Ethics, *In the Matter of Allegations Relating to Representative David Schweikert*, H. Rept. 116-465, 116th Cong. 2d Sess. 6 (2020); *see also Richardson* at 95 (explaining that the public's trust in the integrity of the House is at risk when a respondent demonstrates "such little respect for the internal discipline of the House that [the respondent] would evade its questioning, rather than submitting to the fact gathering process in good faith.").
[141] *Gaetz*.

criminal intent, and noted that he had expressed regret for his conduct. In contrast, in the current matter, there is sufficient evidence of Representative Gaetz's intent to derail the investigation.

The Committee determined that Representative Gaetz's attempts to mislead and deter the Committee from investigating him implicated federal criminal laws relating to false statements and obstruction of Congress. Even if Representative Gaetz's obstructive conduct in this investigation did not rise to the level of a criminal violation, it was certainly inconsistent with the requirement that Members act in a manner that reflects creditably upon the House, in violation of House Rule XXIII, clause 1.

VI. CONCLUSION

Based on the above, the Committee determined there is substantial evidence that Representative Gaetz violated House Rules and other standards of conduct prohibiting prostitution, statutory rape, illicit drug use, impermissible gifts, special favors or privileges, and obstruction of Congress.

VII. STATEMENT UNDER HOUSE RULE XIII, CLAUSE 3(c)

The Committee made no special oversight findings in this Report. No budget statement is submitted. No funding is authorized by any measure in this Report.

VIII. VIEWS OF CHAIRMAN MICHAEL GUEST ON BEHALF OF THE DISSENTING COMMITTEE MEMBERS

I write on behalf of the members of the committee who do not support the release of the report regarding former Representative Matt Gaetz. We believe and remain steadfast in the position that the House Committee on Ethics lost jurisdiction to release to the public any substantive work product regarding Mr. Gaetz after his resignation from the House on November 14, 2024.[142]

While we do not challenge the Committee's findings, we take great exception that the majority deviated from the Committee's well-established standards and voted to release a report on an individual no longer under the Committee's jurisdiction, an action the Committee has not taken since 2006.[143]

House Rules give the Committee jurisdiction over *current* Members, officers, and employees of the House.[144] Consistent with these rules, when a member who is under investigation by the Committee leaves the House, the Committee's standard practice is to close its investigation and make no further statement on its findings. We do not believe the rules authorize the Committee to continue or expand its jurisdiction as it sees fit. Any precedent to the contrary is extremely rare, inconsistent with the rules, and outweighed by the vast majority of matters—too numerous to list—in which the Committee took no material action after losing jurisdiction.

Representative Gaetz resigned from Congress, withdrew from consideration to serve in the next administration, and declared that he would not seek to be seated in the 119th Congress. The decision to publish a report after his resignation breaks from the Committee's long-standing practice, opens the Committee to undue criticism, and will be viewed by some as an attempt to weaponize the Committee's process.

We believe that operating outside the jurisdictional bounds set forth by House Rules and Committee standards, especially when making public disclosures, is a dangerous departure with potentially catastrophic consequences.

Finally, we join the views of the Committee as expressed in its December 23, 2024, public statement addressing the significant and unusual amount of public reporting on the Committee's review of this matter. As expressed by the Committee, "[t]o the extent that any of the public reporting on this matter came from unauthorized disclosures of confidential Committee information, we strongly condemn such unauthorized disclosures, which are damaging and harmful to the Committee's work."[145]

---

[142] 170 Cong. Rec. H5985 (daily ed. Nov., 14, 2014).
[143] Comm. On Ethics, *Investigation of Allegations Related to Improper Conduct Involving Members and Current or Former House Pages*, H. Rept. 109-733, 109th Cong. 2d Sess. Unlike the matter of Representative Gaetz, this 2006 matter *also* involved the conduct of current members.
[144] House Rule 11, Clause 3.
[145] Statement of the Committee on Ethics Regarding Representative Matt Gaetz (Dec. 23, 2024), available at https://ethics.house.gov/press-releases/statement-of-the-committee-on-ethics-regarding-representative-matt-gaetz-2.

www.ingramcontent.com/pod-product-compliance
Lightning Source LLC
Chambersburg PA
CBHW081021240526
45471CB00018B/3925